Joel Stone Ives

The quarto-millennial anniversary of the Congregational church of Stratford, Connecticut

Joel Stone Ives

The quarto-millennial anniversary of the Congregational church of Stratford, Connecticut

ISBN/EAN: 9783337713201

Printed in Europe, USA, Canada, Australia, Japan

Cover: Foto ©ninafisch / pixelio.de

More available books at **www.hansebooks.com**

1639

THE FIRST CHURCH
IN STRATFORD

1889

THE 250TH ANNIVERSARY

OF THE

CONGREGATIONAL CHURCH IN STRATFORD.

At a meeting of the church held May 4, 1888, it was *Voted*, That the Two Hundred and Fiftieth Anniversary of this church be held in the month of September, 1889.

The Standing Committee of the church was appointed a general committee to take charge of the celebration, with power to appoint, from time to time, such sub-committees as might be deemed expedient.

The following is a list of the committees:

GENERAL COMMITTEE OF ARRANGEMENTS.

Rev. Joel S. Ives, *Chairman.*
Deacon A. T. Curtis,
Deacon C. C. Wells,
Deacon S. T. Houghton, *Clerk.*
Deacon S. E. Curtis.
S. T. Palmer,
Carlos D. Blakeman,
Dr. W. B. Cogswell,
James Tracy Richards,
Lewis Burritt.

COMMITTEE ON RECEPTION.

T. B. Fairchild, *Chairman.*
Deacon C. C. Wells,
W. E. Wheeler,
Edwin F. Hall,
Stiles Judson.
Watson H. Smith,
S. T. Palmer,
Wilfred M. Peck,
Henry C. Evans.

COMMITTEE ON ENTERTAINMENT.

Mrs. G. A. Talbot, *Chairman,*   Mrs. R. W. Bunnell.
Mrs. G. H. Spall.

COMMITTEE ON COLLATION.

Mrs. C. A. Tucker, *Chairman*,
Mrs. A. S. Curtis,
Mrs. S. T. Houghton,
Mrs. C. C. Wells,
Mrs. Elbert O. Curtis,
Mrs. C. D. Blakeman,
Mrs. A. T. Curtis,
Mrs. Robert W. Curtis,
Mrs. H. F. Meacham,
Mrs Josiah Booth,
Mrs. Charles W. Blakeslee,
Miss Ada Hubbell.

Mrs. Sylvanus Dickenson.
Mrs. Robert Miller,
Mrs. W. N. Ely,
Mrs. John W. Thompson,
Miss Myra Curtis,
Mrs. S. C. Lewis,
Mrs. Lewis F. Judson,
Miss Mary A. DeVinne,
Miss May Curtis,
Miss Mary Anna Peck,
Mrs. W. A. Stagg.

COMMITTEE ON DECORATION.

Rufus W. Bunnell, *Chairman*,
Horace H. Judson,
Miss Jennie P. Smith,
Miss Alice C. Judson,
F. C. Beach.

Mrs. Howard J. Curtis,
Mrs. W. B. Cogswell,
Miss May L. Smith,
Mrs. J. S. Ives,
Miss Nellie U. Sammis.

COMMITTEE ON MUSIC.

Henry P. Stagg, *Chairman*,
Maynard T. Smith,
Mrs. Emma A. Curtis.

Deacon S. E. Curtis,
Miss Jennie A. Booth.

1639.   PROGRAMME.   1889.

MORNING SERVICE BEGINNING AT HALF-PAST TEN O'CLOCK.

Organ Voluntary, - - - - Mr. Maynard T. Smith.
Doxology. "Praise God from whom all blessings flow."
Invocation, - - - - - Rev. George F. Prentiss.
Anthem.
Reading of Scriptures, - - - Rev. Joseph A. Freeman.
Prayer, - - - - Rev. Charles Ray Palmer, D.D.
Hymn 1312. "O God beneath whose guiding hand."
Historical Address, - - - - Rev. Joel S. Ives.
Hymn 1019. "O, where are kings and empires now?"

Communion of the Lord's Supper.
    Rev. William K. Hall, D.D., and Rev. Franklin S. Fitch.
Hymn 847. "Blest be the tie that binds."
Benediction, . . . By the Pastor.

Collation at the Town Hall at 12.30 o'clock.

AFTERNOON SERVICE BEGINNING AT TWO O'CLOCK.

Organ Voluntary and Anthem.
Prayer, ... Rev. George W. Judson.
Address of Welcome, . - . . . By the Pastor.
Greetings to the Children and Grandchildren of the Church,
Rev. William K. Hall, D.D., and Rev. Franklin S. Fitch.
Response from the First Church of Woodbury,
Rev. J. A. Freeman.
Response from the First Church of Bridgeport.
Rev. C. R. Palmer, D.D.
Response from the Church in Newtown, Rev. J. P. Hoyt.
Hymn 1309. "Great God of nations."
Response from the Church in Huntington. Rev. A. J. Park.
Response from the Church in Trumbull, Dea. H. L. Fairchild.
Response from the Church in Monroe, Dea. W. Wells Lewis.
Hymn. "God of our Fathers."
Written for the occasion by the Pastor.
Response from the Church in Southbury, Rev. David C. Pierce.
Response from the Church in Bethlehem,
Rev. J. P. Trowbridge.
Response from the Church in Washington,
Deacon E. W. Woodruff.
Response from the Church in Roxbury. . . . . . .
Hymn 1030. "Christ is our Corner-stone."
Response from the Church in South Britain, Mr. John Pierce.
Response from the North Church of Woodbury,
Rev. J. L. R. Wyckoff.
Response from the South Church, Bridgeport,
Rev. R. G. S. McNeille.
Hymn 1046. "O God of Bethel."
Response from the Park Street Church, Bridgeport,
Rev. H. C. Hovey, D.D.
Response from the Olivet Church, Bridgeport, J. J. Rose, Esq.
Response from the West-End Church, Bridgeport,
Dea. J. W. Northrop.
Hymn 1141. "Jesus shall reign where'er the sun."
Benediction. . Rev. John G. Davenport.

EVENING SERVICE BEGINNING AT SEVEN O'CLOCK.

Organ Voluntary and Anthem.
Reading of Scripture. - - - Rev. Charles L. Pardee.
Prayer. - - - - - Rev. Alfred E. Ives.
Address. - - - - Rev. William K. Hall, D.D.
Address. - - - - - Rev. Franklin S. Fitch
Hymn 366. "In the cross of Christ I glory."
Reading of Letters, etc.
Address. - - - - Rev. Henry M. Booth, D.D.
Hymn 155. "The peace which God alone reveals."
Benediction. - - - - - - Rev. E. K. Holden.

CHURCH DECORATIONS SEPTEMBER 5TH. (LOOKING WEST.)

This programme,—with the single exception of no response from the church in Roxbury, which did not have a delegate present,—was carried out with prompt exactness.

The exercises commenced punctually at the set time; and the morning services were concluded in season for all to be at the Town Hall at the time appointed for dinner.

The weather was exceptionally fine, neither too warm, nor too cool; a clear sunshiny September day. The various Committees had each so performed the duty assigned to it, that nothing was left undone.

The afternoon services began promptly on time and concluded at about 5 p. m. The readiness, with which the different speakers complied with the request of the committee to observe a time limit, enabled all named on the programme to speak, and there was no manifest weariness in the audience.

Supper was served in the Town Hall at 6 o'clock. Services were resumed at 7, and concluded about 9.

ANNIVERSARY HYMN.

BY REV. JOEL STONE IVES.

God of our Fathers, here we raise
Our grateful hearts in joyful praise;
Thy hand hath led us hitherto,
Thy hand shall lead the journey through.

Two hundred years and fifty more
Since there arose on yonder shore
This ancient church; she lives to-day,
Though centuries have rolled away.

The story of her hopes and fears,
Her struggles, victories, prayers and tears
We tell to-day. The bright'ning page
Unfolds our goodly heritage.

Faith, hope and love can never die;
Recorded are her vows on high.
Unnumbered souls—a glorious throng—
Are witness to our prayer and song.

Hail Ancient Church! Lift high thy voice!
Through centuries yet to come, rejoice!
The Church Triumphant waits, and we
Shall join the immortal company.

The following is a verbatim report of the proceedings.

INVOCATION.

Rev. George F. Prentiss.

Let us invoke the divine blessing.

We render unto Thee, Oh God most High, our most sincere thanks for ancestors who were so clear in their convictions and steady in their testimony; that the mist of the years has not dimmed their conviction, or the clearness of their testimony. We thank Thee that we are this morning permitted to meet, so many of us, in this aged representation of their convictions that we can come and receive the advantage and the benefit of what they have done. Oh God, we thank Thee for Christian fathers and grandfathers of the many generations back. And now, Father, we invoke Thy divine blessing upon this day, upon this celebration, upon this waiting congregation. May all things done here to-day be done to the honor and to the glory of Thy great and holy name. And as Thou didst in the days gone by, help those christians to do their duty well, to honor Thee with all their powers, so do Thou to-day help us to do our duty, to so stand up for the truth and righteousness, as that we shall be loyal to the thought and the conviction of truth and righteousness which is in our own lives. So add Thy blessing to us that what we shall do here to-day may continue in its influence to the generations to come. Do Thou be a God of righteousness and truth and of tender mercy unto our children even to the third and the fourth generation. Do Thou so mold our nation and the thoughts of our men, who are in prominent places, that their truth and their justice may be the truth and justice of God. So influence this nation that all may be transformed into a nation which shall fear God and honor his commandments. Do Thou hasten the time by the fidelity and the loyalty of Thy servants and children here upon earth; hasten the time by this means, when all men shall acknowledge God as Father of all, and King of Kings in all lands. And to the Father, and to the Son, and Holy Spirit we render thanks, not only to-day but in that endless eternity which is to come. Amen.

An anthem by the choir, and the reading of the 89th Psalm, by Rev. J. A. Freeman.

PRAYER.

Rev. Charles Ray Palmer, D.D.

Let us unite in prayer.

Almighty and everlasting God, the hope of Thy Churches, the dwelling place of Thy people in all generations, to the uttermost ends of the earth, we rejoice to call to remembrance Thine eternity. Thy changelessness, in contrast to our transitory lives, and to the many changes by which they are chequered. We rejoice that Thy years have no end and Thy mercies are without number, and from one generation to another Thou art faithful, gracious, full of compassion, slow to anger, plenteous in mercy, giving liberally and upbraiding not. We thank Thee, O God, that in Thy providence the fathers of this church were led to associate themselves together and covenant with one another and with Thee, for the maintaining of the gospel, and for the furtherance of Christian education. We thank Thee from the beginning, through so many generations, Thy favor has preserved this ancient church, and, as we believe, has made it a bulwark of truth and righteousness, a fountain of Christian influence, a blessing unto many. And we praise Thee for all by which Thou hast signalized Thine acceptance of the prayers, the labor and the sacrifices and the offerings of Thy people unto this day. We are reminded of many contrasts between the present and the past, the period seeming so long unto us, although but as yesterday when it is past, unto Thee. We recognize Thy good hand in the continuance of this church unto this time; and we render Thee thanks that Thou hast here educated in Thy fear and in the knowledge of Thy truth and in godliness, so many who have gone hence into various parts of our land, carrying with them Christian knowledge and character to lead useful lives where Thy providence has called them. We thank Thee that there are so many that have here magnified Thy grace, the exceeding gracious words whereon Thou hast caused us to hope in every generation, and that so many have learned here the words wherein they have found eternal life and gone hence to join the Church Triumphant. We cannot but believe with great gratitude they rejoice with us in the memories that are revived this day, and feel a new thankfulness unto God that His grace was revealed unto them here. We pray Thee, Our Father, that these Thy servants, upon whom such an inheritance has descended, may ever be mindful of it. We pray Thee that they may not forget their goodly heritage of Christian tradition, their goodly heritage of Christian memories, their goodly heritage of Christian opportunity; and we pray Thee that every one now connected with this church may feel this day that a new dignity attaches unto his calling in this church and a new burden of responsibility is pressed upon his heart. We pray Thee that Thou wilt continue to establish Thy faithfulness unto those who are here and unto those who shall come after. Show mercy unto Thy servants and salvation unto their children. Here may Thy name be honored, here may Thy truth be testified, here may Thy grace be shown, here may the power of Thy salvation be illustrated for generations that are to come. We praise Thee, O Lord, that we may with so much confidence address ourselves unto Thee. We praise Thee that Thou hast so fully revealed unto us Thy character, that our hearts are filled with confidence and affection towards Thee. O help us to be willing and obedient to Thyself. Help us to be loyal unto our Lord and Saviour, our Prince and the King of righteousness. Help us to be mindful of our own blessed heritage in His everlasting gospel. O that we may, every one of us, feel in the depth of our hearts the power of that gospel, and may our lives be sanctified by means of it, so that we shall show forth the excellencies of Christ our Saviour and hold forth the Word of Life, not only here, but whithersoever Thou shalt lead us in Thy providence. O Lord, our personal hope is in Thee. Our hope is in Thee concerning the families of this people and all the churches that are here represented and all the churches of our land. O Lord, build up Thy kingdom in this nation. Sanctify this nation unto Thyself. Make it a people to Thy praise. Make it a light unto the nations of the earth. Send forth Thy light and Thy truth from it, even unto the ends of the earth, and may the glory of God be revealed until all flesh shall see it. We humbly lay before Thee all the desires of our hearts. Especially do we pray that we may worthily perform whatever rests upon us to do this day, and may we humbly accept all that Thou hast appointed us to do and in all the ways in which Thou shalt lead us. We are mindful that we stand only in the grace of our Lord Jesus Christ; and we lift our hearts rejoicing that He hath made us a priesthood unto God the Father. And in the access which we have unto him by grace do we pray as He taught us in His name: Our Father who art in Heaven, Hallowed be Thy name, Thy kingdom come, Thy will be done in earth as it is in heaven. Give us this day our daily bread, and forgive us our trespasses as we forgive them who trespass against us; and lead us not into temptation, but deliver us from evil: For Thine is the kingdom, and the power, and the glory, forever. Amen.

HISTORICAL ADDRESS.

BY THE PASTOR, REV. JOEL S. IVES.

Since the beginning of the world there never was a time, when history was made so rapidly, as during the lifetime of the present generation; and in all the world no other country has equalled ours in this respect. This fact makes it difficult for us to appreciate the condition of things two hundred and fifty years ago, while it also gives a special interest and value to every effort to bring down into the present the events of the long past and transcribe them for future reference. Since 1876 the historical spirit has been quickened and henceforth American History will take a place of increasing honor in the thoughts of men.

It is with just pride that we contemplate to-day, the long record of this Church of Jesus Christ. It is an honor, not lightly to be esteemed, to be a descendant of this

> "Pure republic, wild, yet strong.
> A 'fierce democracie,' where all are true
> To what themselves have voted;"

and, as well, to serve such a people, where

> "They reverence their priest, but disagreeing
> In price or creed, dismiss him without fear."

Her long story is not now told for the first time. Swan, Cothren, Orcutt, and others also, have been faithful laborers in this field. Whatever of value this discourse may have will be the fulfillment of the Master's word, "others have labored and ye are entered into their labor."

The beautiful shores of Long Island Sound, with the inflowing rivers of sweet water, with the many inlets and land-locked retreats, with the abundant provision for food and clothing, were for untold years the favorite haunts of the North American Indians. The Mohicans appear to have come from the region of the Hudson River to the valley of the Housatonic, which they named Poo-ta-tuck, meaning "falls river," from the falls near Kent, where they made their first camps. Sailing down the river in their canoes, they established camping places till they reached the Sound, and here there was found, by the first Englishmen who came to Stratford, a clan called Cuph eags, which means literally "a place shut in." For how many years this most beautiful haven, formed by the broad mouth of the river and the sheltering arms of Milford Beach and Stratford Point, had been occupied by the red man, it is impossible to say. Their records, though abundant, are rude and vague. But that, as early as 1637, white men had visited these shores, is shown by the testimony of Thomas Stanton, who was for many years the Indian interpreter at Hartford. He declares that the Connecticut colony conquered the Pequots and Pequannocks in 1637 and took hostages from the Pequannock Indians. He also writes that in March of that year they found in Milford "only one house or the karkise of one." In 1638, Roger Ludlow, the brother-in-law of William Endicott, with others, emigrated into Pequonnock and Uncowa. We have, therefore, the record of John Winthrop with his company at Saybrook in 1635; of Mr. Davenport at New Haven in 1638; with earlier expeditions as far as Stamford in 1637 and 1638, while in the spring of 1639, Mr. Prudden and his people settled in Milford, and the same year a number of families settled upon this most "beautiful spot of earth," with whose sacrifices, struggles, achievements, and far reaching results, through two centuries and a half—the Church of Christ of Stratford—our record has to do to-day.

There is no documentary evidence of the organization of this church, as the records to the year 1675 have been lost. But there is abundant circumstantial evidence that the church began its existence as early as 1639, and probably during the summer of that year. I will only take the time to give one item. According to the records of the General Court in October, 1639, this plantation was so far settled that "Sergeant

Nichols" was assigned "to train the men and exercise them in military discipline," and they were given "power to choose seven men from among themselves" who should decide "differences and controversies under 40s." The record also shows that there was a difference between Mr. Prudden and the "Pequonnock plantation" as to the boundaries between them. (Colonial Records i. 36.) It would seem evident that Rev. Adam Blakeman and his company had arrived from Wethersfield before this order of the Court, for without them there would have been too few to meet the conditions of the case. If, therefore, Mr. Blakeman, with a considerable number of families, was here in 1639, there is sufficient reason to put the date of organization in that year, for the sentiment of our fathers was well expressed by John Davenport when he said: "If we build the Lord's house, the Lord will build our house." And as the late Prof. Johnson says in his excellent study of the Commonwealth—Democracy of Connecticut: "It would hardly be too strong to say that the establishment of the town and of the church was coincident: the universal agreement in religion made town government and church government but two sides of the same medal, and the same persons took part in both."

Rev. Adam Blakeman was born in Staffordshire, England, in 1598, and entered Christ's College, Oxford, when nineteen years of age. Cotton Mather writes of him: "He was a useful preacher of the gospel, first in Licestershire, then in Derbyshire, England." A "desirable company of the faithful" followed this "holy man" from England, and by way of Wethersfield came to Stratford as early as 1639, making their settlement at the bend of the creek in Sandy Hollow where the Indians for many years had encamped. Except for this company the settlement seems to have been made by individuals and not by organized association.

Mr. Blakeman's ministry continued till his death, September 7, 1665, at the age of sixty-seven years. Of his writings only his will remains extant, but from a brief notice by Mather, we may be confident of his learning, prudence, and piety. There is this testimony also from Rev. Thomas Hooker, who said of him: "for the sake of the sacred and solemn simplicity of the discourse of this worthy man, if I might have my choice, I would choose to live and die under Mr. Blakeman's ministry." His will makes plain that he was a member of the Synod from 1646 to 1648, which drew up the Cambridge platform, and concerning this he writes that he "could never (through the grace of Christ) see cause to receive any other judgment, nor fall from those principals so solemnly backed with Scripture, and arguments which none yet could overturn."

In 1651, "by the town in public meeting, it was agreed that Mr. Blakeman shall have sixty-three pounds and pay part of his own rate;" which would indicate a good degree of prosperity at that early date. His home was at Sandy Hollow just west of the site of the first Meeting-House. The first Parsonage lot recorded was on Watch Hill, running south to Stratford avenue.

In April, 1655, five months before the death of Mr. Blakeman, the town voted to call Rev. Israel Chauncey "to help Mr. Blakeman in the ministry for a year," and in June, 1666, there was a "mutual agreement for his settling amongst us in Stratford." Mr. Chauncey, the son of Rev. Charles Chauncey, the president of Harvard College, was born in Scituate, Mass., in 1644, and graduated at Harvard in 1661. His studies included medicine and mathematics as well as theology, and during the troublous times of the Narragansett war, he was appointed one of the council of the army, and by this council was ordered to "go forth with the army as their chirurgion." He was actively engaged during the later years of his life in founding Yale College, and November 11, 1701, was chosen the Rector of the institution, but declined the honor, probably on account of failing health, for he died soon after, March 4, 1703. His nephew, Nathaniel Chauncey, who was the first graduate of Yale in 1702, was called, with but one dissenting vote, to the vacant pastorate, but he declined, and for six years the church was without a settled pastor.

Israel Chauncey was a prominent and honored name in the Colony. His ministry of thirty-eight years, including times of war with the Indians, ecclesiastical differences resulting in the division of the church, the building of a new meeting-house, with its change of location, proves not alone his "high reputation for scholarship," but his wisdom in affairs, patience and skill in guiding the thoughts of men, and a "dignity of character" and Christian spirit which secured for himself the respect and honor of all. It is an untold blessing that for more than one-third of a century this church grew up under the influence of such a man. It is the longest pastorate in the history of the church.

From the time of the first call to Mr. Chauncey by the town in April, 1665, there seems to have been a division in sentiment, for at this meeting "word was given to draw to the west side of the meeting-house, and it was clearly evident" that the vote was carried by "the major part." A paper sent to the new pastor in 1666, by the selectmen, calls for a "mutual agreement" in regard to "the preaching of the word and the administering of the sacrament," in accordance with what is known as the "Half-way Covenant" practice. There are also two letters, written in January, and in February, signed by eight men, two of them being also upon the board of selectmen, in which they tell their "loving brethren and friends" that "there hath beene difference about the calling of Mr. Chauncey, and several of us have declared our objections against his settling amongst us till those objections were answered, and we judge they never were unto satisfaction." The "church answer to the men" admits their desire for the "increase and enlargement of ye church when it may be attained in a rulable and satisfactory way," but "plainly" declares "that we cannot at present see how it will stand with the glory of God, the peace of ye church and our and your mutual edification for you to embody with us in this society."

In December, 1666, by the vote of the town, the salary of Mr. Chauncey was fixed at sixty pounds, (this was afterwards increased to one hundred and twelve pounds,) and at the same meeting it was voted to divide the parsonage lot, giving one-quarter part of it to Mr. Peter Bulkley, "or any other man by that party obtained that now endeavors for Mr. Bulkley." Early in 1668, the minority engaged Mr. Zachariah Walker, and the two parties appear to have been recognized upon an equality before the law, although the use of the meeting-house was at first denied them. In 1669 the joint use of the building was approved by the court. But till the spring of 1672 the Second Church of Stratford maintained its existence, at which time "fifteen of Mr. Walker's congregation started with their families for the wilderness of Pomperaug" and formed thus the First Church of Woodbury. No doubt questions other than that of the Half-way Covenant influenced this action, but differences of religious opinion surely were prominent from the beginning.

The following vote of the church, June 4, 1680, would seem to indicate that the church had not before agreed to the practices of the Half-way Covenant. The record is as follows: "At a church meeting the whole consented that baptism be extended to the infants of those qualified according to the 5th prop. of Synod 62."

It seems not to have been easy to settle upon a successor to Mr. Chauncey. Several candidates were voted upon, but for over six years the church did not agree to settle any one as pastor.

During this time, from May, 1703, to March 27, 1707, Mr. John Reed, of Hartford, was hired by the town, although the relations thus maintained seem not to have been satisfactory either to Mr. Reed or to the church.

In June, 1709, seven prominent men were appointed a committee to "seek for a stranger," and September 16th, of the same year, action was taken "for the continuance of Mr. Timothy Cutler amongst us; one hundred and three in favor and none against." The vote for settlement included the building of a house "every way well-finished," a home-lot of over two acres, and one hundred acres of land in the six mile division, as well as a salary of £93. 06s. 8d. All salaries previous to this time appear to have been paid in "products at fixed prices."

Rev. Timothy Cutler was born in Charlestown, Mass., June 1, 1684, and was graduated from Harvard in 1701. He was ordained the third pastor of this church soon after his settlement in September, 1709. He was held in high esteem by all, and bore the reputation of "profound and general learning" as well as being "the most celebrated preacher in the Colony." After a pastorate of ten years he was elected to the presidency of Yale College, and the town with reference thereto "did unanimously signify their grief and sorrow respecting Mr. Cutler's remove from us who under God hath been the happy instrument of uniting us in love and peace after many years of contention." After "passively" submitting to Divine Providence, they were careful to "provide that the Rev. trustees or General Court allow to the town of Stratford one hundred pounds money for and towards the charge of settling another minister among us." Mr. Cutler's home-lot was that now occupied by the "Sterling Homestead," and was the first minister's lot which did not remain the property of his heirs.

After three years' service at Yale, Mr. Cutler announced his preference for the Episcopal church, and in 1723 went to England, where he received the degree of Doctor of Divinity from Oxford University. He died in Boston, at the age of eighty-two years, in which city he had been Rector of Christ's church.

For three years following Mr. Cutler's dismission, Rev. Samuel Russell supplied the pulpit, but a growing party opposed his settlement. An appeal to an Ecclesiastical Council and to the General Court failed to bring relief to the troubled church, but after Mr. Russell left, a day of fasting and prayer was held, and in the spring of 1722, they were able to agree upon Mr. Hezekiah Gold, after having "sat under his ministry with great satisfaction and delight." The letter of acceptance discloses something of the character of the man.

"To ye old Society and Church of Christ in Stratford, to whom grace and peace be multiplied from God our Father and from our Lord Jesus Christ. Dearly beloved, these may inform you of my grateful and thankful acceptance of your generous and honorable proposals for my incouragement in ye great work of ye ministry amongst you, in which I propose to continue as God in his providence shall permit.

Your faithful servant in Christ, during life,

HEZ. GOLD."

His ordination was upon the first Wednesday in June, 1722, and his pastorate continued thirty years with great profit to the church and with large accessions to her membership.

The Ecclesiastical Society, as distinct from the town, in transactions relative to Mr. Gold's settlement, is made plain for the first time on the records. The General Court, in 1717, having passed an act defining the jurisdiction of such societies.

Wide-spread religious interest was awakened throughout New England under the leadership of President Edwards about the year 1735, and Mr. Gold entered heartily into the work, taking a prominent part in the "Great Awakening." During the first year of his ministry sixty were added to the church membership, and between 1731 and 1746 there were two hundred and sixty accessions. Rev. George Whitefield was welcomed by Mr. Gold to his home and pulpit, and the two men were in cordial sympathy, both in doctrine and methods of work. It is probable that the sermon preached by Mr. Whitefield on Monday afternoon, October 27, 1740, from the text: "Turn ye to the stronghold, ye prisoners of hope," was delivered in the open air, for there is a tradition that a Mrs. Burrit, living nearly a mile from Meeting-House Hill, and being at that time in her own yard, heard Mr. Whitefield name his text. Rev. Mr. Swan in his notes, writes: "This sermon was heard by Mrs. Ann Brooks, who narrated the matter to Miss Polly Tomlinson, who related it to me in 1859, and she was so much interested that with her infant in her arms, she went to Fairfield to hear him again the same day." In the following January, Mrs. Brooks united with the church.

These were days of intense feeling and of strong doctrinal preaching, resulting in much discussion, and in the formation of parties, not only in Stratford, but throughout New England. Calvanistic doctrines were re-asserted. A strong opposition was developed to the union of Church and State, as well as to all "New Light Proceedings." It is not strange that difficulties should arise in the path of a pastor in such a time. The opposition found helping influences in the presence of Rev. Richardson Miner, who won a large following, and in other events, which culminated in Mr. Gold's dismission, July 3, 1752.

Before the death of Rev. Adam Blakeman, there were those who remembered the forms of church government in the Church of England, of which they had been members, and during the passing years families came direct from England with the opinions and prejudices of early training. It is not strange, therefore, that upon the differences arising in the settlement of a successor to Mr. Blakeman, the Rev. George Muirson, missionary for the "Society for the Propagation of the Gospel in foreign parts," should find here congenial soil for planting the seeds whence grew the first Episcopal church organization in Connecticut. This was in 1706. After Mr. Cutler left, there were similar disturbing influences and Dr. Samuel Johnson, with marked ability and success, cared for the interests of Episcopacy in Stratford. In the spring of 1714 the churchmen began the work of building a church edifice; but it was not until Christmas Day, 1724, that the building was opened for worship. It was situated within the present Episcopal church-yard.

It is fitting that here some reference should be made to published statements concerning the attitude at this time of Congregational people in the matter of religious tolerance. We do not claim perfection, or that our fathers, having built here for conscience sake, were not strenuous for their privileges; but we are willing to abide by the records. In 1665 the General Court sent word to Charles II., "We know not of any one that hath been troubled by us for attending his conscience, provided he hath not disturbed the public." In 1669 a formal act of religious toleration was put on record. In 1727, the tax for the support of public worship, was by law paid to the minister of the Church of England, by those members living near said church and attending the same; while upon our town records there are receipts of the first Episcopal minister for his share of such annual tax. There is one entry as early as 1730. Any charge that the prisons were full of persecuted Episcopalians is ridiculous and utterly without foundation from any records, except such as may be gathered from the history of Samuel Peters, who married his wife here, and seems to have a special grudge against America in general, and Stratford in particular. Mr. Douglas in his "Summary" of 1749-53, says: "I never heard of any persecuting spirit in Connecticut, in this they are egregiously aspersed." While Bancroft quotes Governor John Haynes, as saying to Roger Williams: "The most wise God hath provided this part of the world, as a refuge and receptacle for all sorts of consciences."

I may here also correct the popular impression that this was ever a Presbyterian church. "An assembly of the ministers of this Colony," at Saybrook in 1666, originated the system of Consociations, which partakes somewhat of the Presbyterian form of church government—indeed, by the irreverant, has been sometimes named "Presbygationalism,"—but the churches remained Congregational, and the consociational system has fallen largely into disuse. This church has always been Congregational in its government, declaring both its autonomy and its fellowship with the churches of like faith and order.

The Rev. Izrahiah Wetmore, the son of Rev. Izrahiah Wetmore, of Stratford, succeeded Mr. Gold, May 16, 1753. His pastorate of twenty-seven years was closed by his resignation in 1780, but from 1785 to his death in 1798, he was settled over the church in Trumbull. He preached the election sermon before the legislature in 1773. This pulpit, during the Revolution, gave no uncertain sound. Mr. Wetmore preached earnestly and boldly for the independence of the Colonies. News of the surrender of Lord Cornwallis to General Washington reached Stratford during the Sabbath service, and was carried immediately to Parson Wetmore, in the pulpit, as he was delivering his discourse. Straightening himself to his full height and making known the intelligence, he said: "It is no place for boisterous demonstrations in the house of God, but we may, in giving three cheers, only go through the motions!"

The inkstand and punch-bowl of this minister of one hundred years ago, are still preserved by his descendants.

The relation of the church to the war of '76 may be told in a word, "That everybody went."

The Church Records are explicit in stating that after April

2. 1780, "the church was vacant four years, four months and two days," but tell us nothing of what transpired during that time, the next item being the minutes of the Council, which convened at the house of Robert Walker, August 3, 1784, for the purpose of ordaining Mr. Stephen William Stebbins, which included "reverend elders and messengers" from New Haven, North Stratford, New Stratford, Ripton, in all twelve churches, as also the former pastor, Mr. Wetmore, showing that the strict rules of the Consociation were not then observed, as more than half of the churches were outside of Fairfield East, and the moderator, Rev. Chauncey Whittlesey, of New Haven, was not the moderator of the Consociation. It was simply a Congregational council.

This was in accord with "articles agreed on and assented to" July 7th, just previous to the ordination. Our manual states that it was a declaration of independency, which seems hardly justified by the record, which reads. "We are of opinion that ecclesiastical councils have no judicial, decisive authority over churches, but yet that it may be of great use in difficult cases and in weighty and important affairs to call in neighboring churches for their advice." The record continues at length to favor the ordaining of pastors by council, and in all matters of church discipline to seek the "consent and concurrence of the brethren," while expressing "charity towards other churches," and willingness that "our ministers should be joined and connected with the association and consociation."

This is not Independency, it is only a protest against the Presbyterian tendency of consociation. It reads to me like good Congregationalism, and it helps to the understanding of this declaration to know that Fairfield East had made just this claim of "power authoritatively and decisively to determine ecclesiastical affairs." It was a wholesome protest.

Our manual also states that the church re-affirmed the Halfway Covenant; which seems hardly just to the records. It will be remembered that this is only thirty years after the difficulties of Mr. Gold's time and the "new light proceedings," which culminated in the division of not a few churches upon the terms of the admission of members, and these "articles," therefore, appear like an effort to harmonize these elements; the fact being that the church did agree upon them. The only resemblance to the principals of the Half-way Covenant was the recognition of infant baptism as bringing such persons to the "next and immediate duty of solemnly" owning such baptism. But note, the articles say: "It is our opinion that none should be admitted hereto, (i. e , the Lord's Supper,) but such as are free from open scandal, appear to be serious, own the Christian doctrines and to the judgment of charity are resolved by divine grace to maintain a conversation becoming the gospel." It is further declared to be "the opinion of this church that as there is but one covenant, the ordinances of baptism and the Lord's Supper are equally sacred;" and that "special pains should be taken to remove the doubts" of any, "and invite and urge them to their duty."

It would certainly be hard to find much fault with this or to show any difference from our present practices, except that we have so much neglected the sacred covenant with Almighty God into which parents enter when they bring their children to Him in the ordinance of baptism.

The records contain the names of one hundred and three persons who were "admitted to special ordinances in the church" during the twenty-nine years of Mr. Stebbins' pastorate. He was dismissed in August, 1813. To him belongs the credit of stopping the vandalism which cut away so much from Academy Hill and spoiled its symetry.

His pastorate covered the times of special religious declension throughout New England In many churches there was not a member who could offer public prayer. War had demoralized the people. French infidelity was rife. Unitarianism and Universalism gained new footholds. The churches of the Pilgrims were in their captivity. But it was the darkness which preceeds the dawn. God was waiting to be gracious to his people.

From the beginning of the history to the end of this pastorate in 1813, the average length of these six pastorates is twenty-six and one-half years. From this time onward the terms of service are to be marked for brevity, that of Mr. Weed being fifteen and one-half years, and no other reaching beyond seven years duration.

There is a tradition that Rev. Jesse Lee preached here July 3, 1789, and it is on record that the first Methodist class was formed May 19, 1790, which in the following year numbered twenty members. Services were held in private houses till 1810, when the first house of worship was built. The present building was erected during the pastorate of Rev. Abram S. Francis in 1839 and 1840.

These gatherings of Methodist people in private houses, for prayer and praise, not only on the Lord's day, but on week-day evenings as well, were the beginnings of similar gatherings among the Congregationalists, who before this time were unacquainted with what we now call the Prayer-Meeting. There were "Circular Fasts," held for twelve or fifteen years after the preaching of Whitefield in 1740, but aside from "The Sacramental Lectures," previous to the communion, whose origin is uncertain, as Prof. Phelps says, "In the olden times the two sermons on the Lord's day, with the accompanying exercises, constituted the whole of the services of public worship." It was not without decided opposition that these prayer-meetings were begun, held first in private houses, then in the shop on Main street, attached to the McEwen house; then in Roswell Curtis' shop; then in the Academy, until it found a resting place in the lecture-room which was built during the pastorate of Mr. Weed in 1845.

Rev. Matthew R. Dutton, September 20, 1814, was ordained the seventh pastor, and for seven years worked successfully for the building of waste places, till in 1821, he accepted the Professorship of Natural Philosophy in Yale College, where he died July 17, 1825.

At this ordination the ordaining prayer was offered by Rev. Nathan Birdseye, a descendant of John Birdseye, the first deacon of this church, who was at this time one hundred years old, and had twelve children, seventy-six grandchildren, one hundred and sixty-three great-grandchildren, and seven great-great-grandchildren—in all two hundred and fifty-eight, of whom two hundred and six were living at the time of his death in 1818, at the age of one hundred and three years, five months, and nine days. Mr. Birdseye's descendants in Stratford, to-day, would comprise a large portion of the village.

So great was the laxity both of faith and practice during the early years of this century, that Mr. Stebbins had refused to administer the communion. After his dismission, at a meeting of the church, June 26, 1814, it was voted "that each member of this church shall manifest his or her assent to the Confession of Faith, adopted by this church, by rising up," and it was further voted, July 24, 1814, that those who thus "assented" shall "constitute the church in this society in Stratford." On the 5th of August, following, Mr. Dutton was called to the pastorate, and there appear to have been eighty members who thus "constituted" the church at this time. During the following year, forty-two were added, on the first Sabbath in July, 1821, seventy, and during the seven years from 1814 to 1825, one hundred and fifty-three.

The records tell us nothing of what happened during the three years following the autumn of 1821, but January 10, 1825, there was "free and cordial unanimity" in calling to the pastorate Rev. Joshua Leavitt, who, though leaving the church after three years to accept the office of Secretary of the American Seaman's Friend Society, was a most active and aggressive man in affairs both of Church and State, and exerted a strong influence in the town especially upon the questions of temperance, the emancipation of the slaves, and the conduct of the schools.

February 27, 1828, sixty delegates representing thirty-six churches, met here in general conference. There were addresses to the church, heads of families, the aged, the impenitent, and the youth. In Mr. Leavitt's own words, "The whole exercises were very solemn, and a crowded house was deeply impressed by the scene. May the savor of that day long remain in Stratford."

If all of the clerks and pastors had kept the records as Mr. Leavitt did there would be no lack of data for the use of the future historian. After transcribing the full details of his dismission, he puts on record the following: "And now that my pastoral connection with this people is thus formally dissolved, I give up my charge into the hands of Him from whom I received, with the humble prayer that grace, mercy and peace, from God our Father, and our Lord Jesus Christ, may be multiplied unto them forevermore. May God reward them a thousand fold for all their kindness to me and mine, and in His own good time and way send them a more faithful and successful minister." The spirit of a faithful pastor breathes through every word of this benediction.

Dr. Leavitt, in 1826, organized the Sunday-School and was its superintendent during the remainder of his pastorate, with the assistance of Miss Mariah McEwen, who, upon Mr. Leavitt's resignation, took full charge of the school for several years, till the election of Eli Booth, who was followed in succession by Deacon David P. Judson, Henry Plant, William Strong, Henry Plant, a second term, Frederick Sedgewick, Deacon Samuel T. Houghton, Deacon Samuel E. Curtis, Rev. Joel S. Ives, Principal Wilfred M. Peck, and the present incumbent, Horace H. Judson.

June 18, 1826, after a reference of the matter to a committee appointed in the preceding May, a standing committee, or "Helps," were elected, consisting of Deacon Agur Curtis, Deacon Philo Curtis, and Deacon Agur Curtis, 3d.

Rev. Thomas Robbins was installed pastor in 1830, but was dismissed in September of the following year. Rev. Samuel Griswold seems to have supplied the pulpit for a time, as thirty-two were received by him to this church in December, 1831, and January, 1832.

The tenth pastor was Rev. Frederick W. Chapman, who was ordained September 5, 1832, and remained six and a half years. These were times of widespread revival interest, and names were added to the church roll who have been a tower of strength; exerting an influence of blessing upon the community, especially in Putney and Oronoque. Prayer-meetings were begun in Oronoque, during the pastorate of Dr. Dutton, and there have been prayer-meetings at the Putney chapel since 1867. The chapel in Putney was built in 1844.

These religious influences have been a large factor in making those communities thrifty and wholesome.

The last half century of our history began with a pastorate cherished in the memory of all whose recollections reach back thirty-five years or more, and fruitful in all good things to this church and community. December 4, 1839, Rev. William Bouton Weed was ordained pastor and ministered to this people fifteen and one-half years, till his dismission in May, 1855, to accept the pastorate of the First church in Norwalk, where, "having served his generation by the will of God, he fell on sleep," December 13, 1860.

I can do no better than to quote a paragraph from the tribute of Dr. Robert R. Booth, who said at Mr. Weed's funeral: "It was at Stratford that his ministeral character was formed, his peculiar reputation was acquired, and his great work was done. He went there a young man, with a mind richly stored with learning, and a heart all aglow with Christian fervor. He burst like a new planet upon this quiet village, where preaching had before been exhibited more as a sober, sacred duty, than as a divine and thrilling art. From the very beginning of his service there, he revealed himself as a remarkable man and his fame went abroad into the adjacent country. A glorious revival of religion followed soon, coming like the warm breath of spring to unlock the ice-bound earth and fill all hearts with gladness. Many precious souls were then gathered into the church. His whole course was signalized by the most laborious study, by ardent and devoted labors, and by a remarkable earnestness of action, truthfulness and plainness of speech, and an intense force of life which made him the central influence of the town. His sermons were always driven home. His views of truth and duty became the standards of opinion. Men of all conditions and of all varieties of views were attracted to his pulpit, and, notwithstanding the eccentricities of his character, he has left an impression for good upon that community which will not pass away while the generation that knew him continues on the stage of action."

Rev. Joseph R. Page was installed February 11, 1857, and

was dismissed September 26, 1858; the "only reason for making the request" for dismission, in Mr. Page's own words, "is the want of adaptation to each other of the parties." The records seem to show good work and fifty names were added to the church roll during this brief pastorate.

After a unanimous call, Rev. Benjamin L. Swan entered upon his duties as pastor, November 1, 1858, and was dismissed after about four years and one-half of service, during which time the present house of worship was completed and the general work of the church seems to have been thoroughly attended to. Mr. Swan's records are models both in matter and penmanship, and his interest in the history of the church and town wrought results of incalculable value. It seems most unfortunate that this pastorate could not have been greatly extended. And to our brother whose life we trust may long be spared and whose presence at this anniversary was much desired, we extend our heartiest greetings with our appreciation of the labors of love here performed.

With characteristic exactness there is recorded the facts of having preached in this pulpit one hundred and ninety-five Sabbaths, and six hundred and ninety-six sermons and lectures; of thirty-seven admitted to the church, and of nine hundred and eighty-three "calls on families," which numbered one hundred and sixty in 1859, and one hundred and seventy-seven in 1862.

The following resolution was adopted by the church: "In accepting the resignation of our pastor, Rev. B. L. Swan, we take occasion to express to him our high appreciation of his gifts and learning and our unhesitating confidence in his piety and soundness in the faith, and that we affectionately assure him of our sincere wishes and our prayers for his usefulness and happiness in whatever sphere God in His providence may hereafter place him."

May 25, 1864, Rev. Louis E. Charpiot was installed pastor, the sermon being preached by Dr. Noah Porter, and during the two years that he ministered twenty-five were added to the church.

William K. Hall, D.D., after theological studies in New

Haven and in Germany and ordination as chaplain of the Connecticut volunteers, was installed pastor of this church October 24, 1866, and was dismissed May 21, 1872; a letter of resignation having been sent to the church March 31st, which stated, to quote Dr. Hall's words, "the discouragements under which I was pursuing my work among them, from a want of their coöperation in that work."

In July, 1867, "It was voted that the public services of the afternoon be omitted and that public worship be held in the evening." For nineteen years the plan of holding the second service in the evening during several months in the summer and in the afternoon during the rest of the year was continued, with something of friction whenever the votes were taken, till November 14, 1886, when it was voted to hold the second service in the evening during the entire year.

In 1869 a manual was issued which shows a membership of two hundred and sixty-six; during the year previous forty-three were added to the church. The church is greatly to be commended for issuing so much of historical matter which had been gathered by the research of Rev. Mr. Swan. A second manual was issued in 1881, in which were added pictures of the present edifice and of the edifice preceding this, and, also, a list of members from the beginning, gathered with great patience and labor by Mr. C. H. Warner. The membership of the church was then two hundred and seventy.

Dr. Hall accepted a call from the First Presbyterian church in Newburgh, N. Y., in January, 1873, and is still ministering to that people with increasing usefulness.

April 6, 1873, a call was extended to Mr. Frank S. Fitch, who was about to graduate at Yale Theological Seminary. June 17th, he was ordained pastor, and ministered with great acceptance and marked success till September 29, 1878, when he resigned to accept a call from the Seventh Street Congregational church in Cincinnati. These were years of revival, and one hundred and twenty-six were added to the church, making at the present time about one-quarter of the membership. "He that winneth souls is wise." It has always seemed to me extremely unfortunate that after receiving this large

3

company of young people to the church Mr. Fitch could not have remained to train them in Christian work and establish them in the faith.

Samuel Howard Dana, D.D., was called to this pastorate December 22, 1878, and was installed March 12, 1879. At his own request he was dismissed December 6, 1881. The following is from the "Result of Council":

"In reluctantly consenting to sanction the removal of Mr. Dana from the fellowship with the churches of this body to which he was cordially welcomed nearly three years since, and in which he has been increasingly appreciated, we tender him our heartiest wishes for his future welfare and usefulness, and we commend him to the churches in the midst of which his lot may be cast hereafter, as an active, earnest and diligent minister of Christ, of Catholic spirit, of fine culture and scholarly aspiration; of unblemished character and in good repute as a preacher and pastor; and as a man whose patience and dignity in peculiar trials have been recognized with admiration both by the people of his immediate charge and by the Christian public surrounding them."

For the past six years Dr. Dana has been the successful pastor of the Union Congregational church of Quincy, Illinois. We are sorry not to have him with us in these festivities.

During the six months, beginning with February, 1882, Dr. Edwin Johnson supplied the church, and during the summer Rev. F. S. Fitch, to whom a unanimous and hearty vote was extended to assume again the pastorate. In declining Mr. Fitch wrote, "My heart has said 'yes' all along, but my judgment has constrained me to say 'no.'"

Early in 1883, H. M. Ladd, D.D., supplied for several weeks and a call was extended to him, which he declined. As the year wore on many candidates were heard, till September 23, 1883, a call was extended to your present pastor, whose term of service is, by a few months, longer than any since that of Mr. Weed. Meanwhile the membership of the church had been growing less, from two hundred and seventy to two hundred and fifty, but since 1884, eighty have been added, making the number about the same as during Mr. Hall's and

Mr. Fitch's ministry. Oh that the Lord might visit his heritage in blessing and fit pastor and people for a large ingathering of precious souls!

October 26, 1885, a Young People's Society of Christian Endeavor was organized and has been a most hopeful and helpful means of bringing the young people into the Christian life and of training them for Christian service. For more than a year a Junior Society has been found useful in fitting the little ones for work, and in encouraging them in looking forward to helpful participation in the activities of the church.

Philip Groves' name appears among the earliest lists of the Colony. He was the only Ruling Elder of the church; in 1654 he was chosen "Assistant," and "was empowered to marry persons." The following is the list of Deacons: John Birdsey, whose son, John, was born in Stratford in 1641; Timothy Wilcoxson, Thomas Wells, Robert Walker, John Thompson, Ephraim Judson, Job Peck, Elnathan Wheeler, Isaiah Brown, Ebenezer Coe, Nathan McEwen, Samuel Ufford, Agur Curtis, Philo Curtis, Agur Curtis, "3d," David P. Judson, Agur Treat Curtis, Lewis Beers, Charles C. Wells, Samuel T. Houghton, and Samuel E. Curtis.

The first house of worship was on the shore of the creek at Sandy Hollow, where is now the barn belonging to Captain William Barrymore. There are no records of its dimensions, but if it was like the first meeting-house in New Haven, it was square, with a hip-roof, and on the top an out-look against the approach of Indians, and, also, some provision for a bell, which is said to have been the first church bell in the State. The first sexton and bell-ringer was John Peet; when his duties began we do not know, but in 1660 John Pickett was elected by the town to fill his place. In 1661 "it was agreed that there shall be a gallery builded in the meeting-house in the convenient place." This house was in use about forty years, for in 1681 it was torn down and the materials sold at auction; some of the timbers being in the house near by, now occupied by Mr. Joseph Savage.

"Goodman Peake" and "Goodman Pickett" not only cared

for the building and rang the bell for meetings and at "nine of the clock," but were required "to watch over the disorderly persons in the meeting and use his discretion in striking any person whom he finds so disorderly."

As the years went on the population of Stratford moved "up town." So that in 1678, when the location of the new church, which had been resolved upon only two years after the Narragansett war, was mooted and five different localities were mentioned. Rev. Israel Chauncey agreed to give £40 if they would "sett the meeting-house upon the hill," and November 25, 1679, it voted to "move up town."

The location, which we call Academy Hill, was then Watch-house hill and in early years marked the northern boundary of the settlement, as along the northern brow of the hill there was a row of palisades, within which was the Watch-house. The dimensions of this second meeting-house were "forty-eight feet in length, forty-two feet in breadth, and sixteen feet between joints," from which I judge that the general appearance of the building was the same with the first. The building committee were "Captain William Curtis, Sergt. Jerem. Judson, John Curtis, Sergt. Jehiel Preston, and John Birdseye, Jr." The house was built during the summer of 1680, and by vote of the town the inhabitants were seated according to rules of dignity, one special rule being the amount they paid to the new building, which was of course by tax and not voluntary. At this time a day's work was credited at two shillings and sixpence to three shillings.

The tax which was voted "to pay charges about the building" was £100. In 1689 it was voted to fortify the house so that it could be used "as a place of security for women and children."

In 1700 an end gallery was built, and in 1715 two side galleries, and it was voted in 1718 that the west side gallery "shall be seated with married men, the east gallery with married women, and antiant bachelors and antiant maidens the second seats." In 1715 "farmers were granted liberty to erect suitable shelter for their horses on all public days." The first pews were built about 1710.

INTERIOR OF OLD CHURCH.

During the pastorate of Mr. Gold, on the "second Monday, February, 1743. voted that it is necessary to build a meetinghouse." This is the action of the ecclesiastical society, not the town. There was also a difference of opinion in regard to location. for "Captain Theoplius Nichols, Mr. Robert Walker, Jr., and Sergeant Daniel Porter," were empowered to make application to the General Assembly for "a committee to fix a place where the said society shall erect their meetinghouse." The dimensions were to be sixty feet in length, forty in width, the posts twenty-six feet, and a steeple one hundred and thirty feet high. This third meeting-house was located near the sight of the old academy, a few rods west of the preceding house, facing south, where was the door of entrance, and some marks of the bridle-path leading to it now remain. It was destroyed by lightning June 11, 1785, the fire bursting out first from the steeple. This was during the pastorate of Mr. Stebbins.

The society seem not at all to have been disheartened by their loss, for the frame of the new house was begun to be raised on Friday, May 17, 1786, upon this location where we now are, which was then called Hiell's hill, and also Smith shop hill, and in just twenty-five weeks it was completed, the services of dedication being on Sunday, November 12th, when Mr. Stebbins preached in the morning from Psalms 107:7, after which was the communion, and at three in the afternoon there was a union service, at which time Mr. Stebbins again preached.

The dimensions of this fourth building were the same as the third, and the general appearance is familiar from the cut in our manual. It was an imposing structure for the times. The view of the interior has been preserved through the thoughtfulness of Mr. R. W. Bunnell, who stepped into the building November 1, 1858, as it was being torn down to make way for the present edifice, and sketched the pulpit, soundingboard and surroundings so perfectly that the room has been finely reproduced. Mr. Swan records that six hundred and twenty-four were received to the church membership in that building.

Mr. William A. Booth, of New York, then living here, built the beautiful parsonage, which each pastor since Mr. Swan has greatly enjoyed, and for several years rented it to the society for a nominal sum. It was afterwards purchased of him. He was largely instrumental in the erection of the present meeting-house, which was dedicated October 27, 1859, with the scripture reading by Dr. Brace, of Milford; the prayer by Dr. Hewitt, of Bridgeport, and the sermon by Dr. R. S. Storrs, of Brooklyn. Its architecture is peculiarly ecclesiastical and beautiful. Last year it was greatly improved by the introduction of steam heating apparatus, as well as thoroughly repaired.

The town meeting has frequently been referred to as the corner-stone of our civil freedom. Too much honor cannot be given to Connecticut as the mother of our democracy and the author of our widespread doctrine of civil government as well as the source of the compromise out of which grew our present National Constitution, in which Stratford had her honored part; but beyond this I agree with Senator Platt in the declaration, that "The Congregational church was a religious democracy, and our civil independence and political self-government are its necessary out-growth. The day of the meeting-house was a day of moral earnestness."

The metrical version of the Psalms, by Sternhold and Hopkins, was printed with the Bibles of the latter part of the 16th century, and was probably used by the founders of this church. The Bay Psalm Book was published in 1640, and after a few years was in general use in New England. It is interesting to remember that at the organization of this church the King James verson of the Bible was not in universal use. The Genevan Bible was used for many years at New Haven, and not unlikely in this church, also, with the same strong opposition to "any change in the Word of God," which we find to-day with reference to the Revised Version. Dr. Watt's Scriptural selection was in use after the Bay Psalm Book and, also, Tate and Brady, which was also published in 1765 with an appendix from Dr. Watts. A hundred years after this we find the Church Psalmody, and in 1857 there was in use here the "Psalms and Hymns," issued by the State Association. In February, 1873, a committee was appointed who selected the "Songs for the Sanctuary," which has been in use since then. In early years one or more choristers were elected who set the tune with a pitch-pipe; after that the base viol and other stringed instruments led the service of song, with the addition of a choir completing the four parts. Fugue tunes came into use in the latter part of the 18th century. The next advance was a melodeon with two banks of keys, and in 1868 our present organ was purchased.

"All nations prayse the Lord; him prayse
all people. For his mercies bee
great toward us; also always
the Lord's truth lasts, the Lord prayse yee."
[From Bay Psalm Book, 1640.]

In this brief time, which can be taken from the crowded exercises of this anniversary, I have given a few meagre outline touches along the two hundred and fifty years of our history. The simple facts would be of little interest were it not that a "master thought" underlies them all. It is, *What God has wrought through His people for His kingdom.* The workmen—more than two thousand of them, members of this church—have died, but the work dies not. The star of hope never shined more brightly. The hastening glory of the coming kingdom is beyond the dawning, it climbs toward the zenith of its consummation. We have been considering the history of our church, but we are a part of a great whole. There is a wider sweep of historic forces—there is the universal church of God. And although our Congregational churches do not yet number their membership in the millions, we do take pride in the contributions which we have made to the past and in that which we are williang to make to the more glorious future. Our freedom of worship, our liberty of thought, our protest against any hierarchy, our equality before God—"the common priesthood of believers"—our zeal for the Kingdom of Righteousness and Truth,—these are the truths which our fathers gave us, and these are the things which we would bear onward to the church of Christ universal. "For yet a very little while He that cometh shall come," and in that triumphal glory we shall have our share, while to Him that sitteth upon the throne and unto the Lamb shall be the everlasting praise.

COMMUNION.

Rev. W. K. Hall., D.D.

St. Paul said, That which I have received give I unto you. On the same night in which our Lord was betrayed he took bread and blessed it. In imitation of our Lord's example let us look now for the Divine blessing upon this bread.

Almighty Father, it is with a holy joy and devout thanksgiving that we gather around the table of our Lord to-day. We are thankful for the past. We are thankful for the fathers' faith, and the fathers' love, and the fathers' service, thankful to Thee for their consecration to Christ and to His service. We are conscious to-day of receiving not simply a heritage of circumstances, a heritage of knowledge, a heritage of truth from them, but a heritage of life, a life that was fed upon the Christ upon whom we feed to-day. We are thankful, our Heavenly Father, that we are possessors of this life, that has been communicated to us down through the centuries, and we rejoice to-day in the same truth in which our fathers rejoiced; and to-day we are having the same comforts and the same source of peace and strength, and the same inspiration for high purpose and earnest work, here at the table of our Lord. Amid all the changes of the changing years we gather around this table conscious that the significance of the symbol that is now before us has remained unchanged; that He is the same yesterday, to-day, and forever; that the cross that was once up-lifted, and the Christ, who once gave Himself to redeem the world, are the same, and so upon the same food we eat to-day as our fathers did. And grant, and grant now, we pray Thee,

---

Note.—The following officiated at the Communion: Deacons R. B. Lacey, J. H. Lindsley, W. Wells Lewis, E. W. Woodruff, A. L. Winton, A. T. Curtis, and C. C. Wells.

that the blessings with which Thou didst bless them, the blessings of spiritual strength, the blessings of hope, of life, of comfort, of peace, of joy, may be ours to-day. And we would, our Father, not simply look back upon the past or cast our eye down the future; and while we are thankful for the past, which has been bequeathed to us, with all its rich legacies and ever-constant power for good, thankful to Thee for the presence in which we stand, we pray for blessings upon the children and the children's children that may come after us; that the light here may continue to shine, giving forth no uncertain light, and that this table, with its blessed significance, may continue to give nourishment and strength to those, who shall come after. May there be loyalty, truth and allegiance to Christ and love for Him. And may we hear the voices from this high day of festivity and joy, with renewed purpose to serve Thee, with renewed consecration prompted by Thy love shed abroad in our hearts by the Holy Ghost; and, denying all ungodliness and worldly lusts, may we live righteous and godly in this present world, looking unto the blessed hope and glorious appearing of our great God and our Saviour Jesus Christ, who gave himself for us, that he might redeem us from all iniquity and purify unto himself a peculiar people, zealous of good works. And to the name of the Father, Son and Holy Ghost, be praise forever. Amen.

And when our Lord had blessed the bread he gave it unto his disciples, saying, This is my body broken for you. Take, eat. This do in remembrance of me.

REV. F. S. FITCH.—He also took the cup and gave thanks.

WE thank Thee, our dear Father in Heaven, for Thy love wherewith Thou has loved us, and for all these efforts which Thou hast been making for our salvation. We thank Thee especially for the gift of Thy dear Son, our Lord and Saviour Jesus Christ, through whom we have remission of sins and newness of life and access to Thee. We beseech Thee that Thou wilt fill our hearts with gratitude to the Holy Spirit for this gift of our Lord; and as we receive this fruit of the vine, may we understand Thy measure of infinite love; for greater love hath no man than this, that a man lay down his life for his friend. May we be able to discern his wounded body, his broken life, his agony, his death: Who, though he was no sinner, stood in our place and suffered as our surety. Help us also, our Heavenly Father, to have a due sense of our own unworthiness. May we realize that, if our disease was so fatal that no other remedy would avail, that sin must be a great terror to our souls. May we understand that, without the remission of blood through our Lord and Saviour Jesus Christ, there is no salvation, and may we therefore gladly acknowledge our indebtedness to Him who hath made this costly sacrifice for us. Wilt Thou set apart for holy uses so much of this fruit of the vine as we shall drink, that it shall not be a type of the world's greatest debauchery and sin, but that it shall be a type to us of the vine and the branches, of that impartation of life which strengthens us here and makes immortality possible. We beseech Thee as we receive this cup that we may receive it as a token of Thy grace and to the honor of the Lord Jesus. Amen.

BENEDICTION.

REV. JOEL S. IVES.

AND now, the God of peace, who brought again from the dead our Lord Jesus, the great Shepherd of the sheep, through the blood of the everlasting covenant, make you perfect in every good work to do His will, working in you that which is well-pleasing in His sight, through Jesus Christ our Lord, to whom be the glory forever and ever. Amen.

Recess for collation at Town Hall.

COLLATION TABLES IN TOWN HALL.

THE DIVINE BLESSING WAS INVOKED BY
REV. H. A. DAVENPORT.

Our Father, God: we want Thy blessing at this family table of the household of faith. We thank Thee for the brightness and fellowship of this day. We thank Thee for Thy favor to us in spiritual and temporal matters. We, therefore, earnestly crave thy blessing, that Thou wouldst sanctify these comforts and these pleasures and this sweet Christian communion. Be gracious to us this hour, we pray Thee, and accept our thanks, in Jesus Christ. Amen.

AFTERNOON SERVICE.

PRAYER.

REV. GEORGE W. JUDSON.

LET us pray.

Thou hast been our dwelling place, O Lord, in all generations. Before the mountains were made, before Thou didst form the earth and the world, even from everlasting to everlasting, Thou art God. And yet we rejoice to know Thee as our Heavenly Father, and we rejoice to acknowledge Thy presence in these last festivities, and in these joyful memories. Accept then, we pray Thee, the gratitude and the thanksgiving of our hearts for all the mercies and blessings which, in all the days that have gone by, Thou hast bestowed upon this ancient church. We rejoice in the character of Christian piety and fervent enthusiasm of those who established this church. We rejoice in the work which was done by all those who followed in the footsteps of the founders of this church. We rejoice for Christian fathers and mothers. We rejoice for Christian homes. We rejoice in all the lives of beneficence and influence in this place that have been lived, showing forth not the glory of self, but the glory of Christ. We do thank Thee for the children which have gone forth, in the days that have gone, from the maternal roof, in the midst of other surroundings, continuing the good work which they were permitted here to begin. And we do beseech Thee that, as children and the children's children have gathered to-day in the old home, Thy blessing may rest upon us; and that those, who shall bring the tributes of their love and their affection, may be able to give adequate expression to the gratitude and love of their hearts. Now bless us, we beseech Thee, in the especial services of this afternoon. Grant that the welcome home may make us feel, each and every one of us, at home in our fellowship with one another, and in our communion with Thee, our common Lord. Grant, we beseech Thee, that the word spoken unto us by former pastors of this church may come to us bringing to our minds the remembrance of services which they were permitted here to do for Thee, and may the remembrance of these services add impressiveness and power to the words of counsel which they shall bring to us, and as those churches, which are here represented, shall bring one by one the tidings and the messages of their love and affection, may it be that a tide of love for Thee shall fill all our hearts, for Thee, the giver of these good gifts, for Thee, the inspirer of all this Christian endeavor, and thus may it be that the services of this hour shall do us all good, shall stimulate and quicken us in our Christian endeavors, shall inspire us in all that we have to do in following the Master, that we may be able so worthily to serve Thee with all the Israel of God, that not only Thy kingdom shall come but Thy will be done in earth as it is done in heaven. We ask it in the name of our Lord and Master. Amen.

ADDRESS OF WELCOME,

By the Pastor.

The grandmother is keeping house to-day; and she finds herself somewhat in the position of that mother of our nursery rhymes, who had so many children that she didn't know what to do! But we are here to give you a most hearty welcome;—you who are the children and the grandchildren of this ancient church. We are here to bid you most hearty welcome who come as friends, and who come in remembrance of the ancestors who have lived in this church. We bid you most hearty welcome. It is our rejoicing that you are with us to-day. We are glad because the years have rolled around till this anniversary has been reached, and in this joyous occasion we can thus celebrate our Quarto-Millennium. Yet this upon the programme which you read, "Address of Welcome by the Pastor," was put on simply to fill up and make the programme look well. It wasn't intended that there should be any set address. We are rejoicing that two of the former pastors of this church are present with us, and it devolves upon them to give the greetings to these children and grandchildren who are with us to-day. We are glad now to listen to Dr. Hall.

GREETINGS TO THE CHILDREN AND GRANDCHILDREN OF THE CHURCH.

REV. W. K. HALL, D.D.

I SUPPOSE it was the intention simply to fill out the programme. It is so short!

I have been looking at these panels and have been wondering, my dear brother, whether it was for to-day you have had so many panels put in this church, so that at the time of this celebration there would be just so many churches' names to fill in.

MR. IVES. We are just one child short and had to put up that flag.

DR. HALL. You haven't heard from all of them.

It is about a score of years ago, twenty years next May, if my memory serves me rightly, this dear old grandmother was invited to participate in the birthday exercises of her first-born child, the Woodbury church; and I have been requested by your pastor to limit my words to greetings to the Woodbury church and her children. As I read that request, my mind went back twenty years ago to the lovely feast we held up among the hills and by the beautiful river, with this bright, beautiful, fair daughter two hundred years old I was then a young man just entering the ministry, and I was called upon to represent this old grandmother; and the sentiment at that time proposed to which I was called upon to respond was this, or something like it: "Venerable mother: Thou that dwellest by the sea, called in thy green old age to celebrate the birthday of thy first daughter, we greet thee and we welcome thee to this fair heritage with which the Lord our God hath blessed thee."

That is pretty good for the memory of one who is called

upon to represent a church that was then about two hundred years old. At that time this daughter, and the children and grandchildren that were then with her, in the course of the day's festivities, referred to the time which would not be far away. It seemed to me then to be very far away, when we would assemble beneath the old homestead roof and celebrate the Two Hundred and Fiftieth Anniversary of the mother's life. The years have gone by, dear friends, and those of you who were with us at Woodbury perhaps think it was only yesterday we had the lovely pleasant time together. How heartily we entered into the rejoicings of that day! While this mother has had, I think, about five children, this daughter has had five, and a granddaughter: so that she is not simply a grandmother but a great-grandmother; for, if I mistake not, the church in South Britain is the grand-child of the church in Woodbury. Am I right?

MR. IVES. I don't know, sir.

DR. HALL. I thought you were the historian.

MR. IVES. Not of that church.

DR. HALL. I think the South Britain church was a grandchild of the church of Woodbury. If so, the old church here is a great-grandmother instead of a grandmother. We greet and welcome you, dear child of Woodbury, and your children and your grandchildren to-day. You see your own mother hale and hearty as ever. There is no sign of decrepitude or decadence about her. It is one sad thing when we come to visit our parents in declining years to find marks that make us sad. We see the deep furrows in the face, we see the tottering step, we see the failing faculties; and it is sometimes far more saddening than joyous to see an old parent from whom we have been separated perhaps many years. But not so with the church of the living God. If she is fulfilling her mission, doing the work that God has assigned her, she grows youthful with the years; and, though the years wax and wane, she seems to take on with increasing years increased vitality. And so to-day this old church of Christ presents as fresh a life, as buoyant a heart, as sprightly a step, as any of her children. And as you draw nearer to her, and receive her warm congratulations and greetings to-day, beneath the old roof, by the old fireside, the daughters, and the daughters' children, there come the evident tokens of a life prosperous, strong and vigorous. You find one who is as true to-day to the standards of the faith as when, two hundred and fifty years ago, the few gathered together to sign with their own hands the solemn covenant. Your mother has never desired one verse less in the Bible. She has never abbreviated her creed, nor has she shortened the commandments. Faithful to truth: and although she may have an increase of knowledge above that of the fathers, yet still she looks back with reverence and with devout thanksgiving to the grace of God that hath crowned the years, and looks forward with bright, keen eye to the future, believing that, as long as yonder river flows to the sea, and as long as yonder waves beat upon the shore, though the old town of Stratford, with its historic records and glories, may be engulfed within the more modern but prosperous, busy city of Bridgeport. that is continually grasping from her old reach and domain; and though she may lose possibly in the years to come, her very name; yet, while this church of Christ stands, it will stand by the truth of God, it will stand by the old symbols the fathers have handed down to her, faithful to the end. And so she bids you, children and grandchildren, as you leave her fold to-day, to go back to your own homes and own fire-sides, to take back with you the spirit of vitality, that you breathe in anew as you come to these old haunts of your youth, of the years long gone by. But I remind myself that I am to speak but five minutes, and I think I must have spoken five minutes and a half.

MR. IVES. You will now hear a response from the oldest daughter.

RESPONSE from the First Church of Woodbury,

REV. J. A. FREEMAN.

As representing this daughter to-day, I say, Here are we and those whom God has given us. We do rejoice to be present with you to-day, and to speak this word of congratulation. I think perhaps it may be well when I commence to let you down just a little: we have been going up pretty well. But the element of brevity comes in here, and this saying I have heard: "Be learned or unlearned; formal or informal, wise or unwise, only be brief." We will all be brief, dear friends, we will all be brief. There is something, however, to say that I think is very important now, in reference to the relation this daughter, that has gone out from Stratford, has to the old mother; and it seems to me that the relation is not very different from what the relation between the mother and her children always is. I look around and about on these panels, and I see these different names, and I remember many years ago the oldest daughter going out from home, and coming back, after the years were past, with her children. We come to-day to congratulate, to be one with you. What is the use of it all? What is the use of a daughter going to California, or Washington Territory, or Oregon, or any of those places? What is the use? Why are not the daughters and all the granddaughters here in Stratford? Why haven't they lived here through the years up to the present moment and enjoyed the society of mother and grandmother? Why, it is the same old story, illustrated by us, illustrated by the grandchildren, illustrated all the time, the eagle stirring up the nest and the young being turned out of the old place to find their new homes and fulfill their destiny. So up among the hills two hundred and twenty years ago almost, the daughter went for better or for worse; and the hills in the Pomperaug valley now see a change, the hills feel the influence of the separation that came two hundred years and more ago. They feel that influence whether Calvinist, Presbyterians, or this, that and the other, what the difference? It is God's way, it is God's way, putting down his hand into the nest and stirring up the nest, and the young birds go, and there are new homes, and you see the results of it all.

Now, there is one thing that I want to say, to-day, that we can boast about a little when we come back. These children you have spoken of so well—now there are children to show for themselves. They are a very modest people—

Dr. HALL. They get that from the grandmother.

Mr. FREEMAN. Yes, they get it from the grandmother. They are very modest, very modest indeed. They are all very modest, especially the youngest daughter: the youngest granddaughter is very modest indeed. They are all modest, nice children; they are all nice children, all clean, all do just right. We have brought them back here. As a matter of fact, in reference to what you have said, there is not a daughter, neither of these daughters I believe, certainly not this one and the daughter of this one on the hills, that has ever let down the great principle of the mother here in this church, not one of them; and they have lived there, and they have touched that whole region, and they have carried the principles of which we have heard to-day in that whole region. Daughter,— Woodbury First Church, 1670, and grandchildren, with their names around in this house on these different panels, they are not ashamed to come back here, to-day, and speak of what they are, as related to the mother and the principles they have held through all these years.

Mr. IVES. Mr. Hall has taken the Woodbury Church with the children. We shall now hear a greeting from Mr. Fitch to the rest of the family.

REV. F. S. FITCH. I remember some sixteen years ago as a theological student in my senior year, at the invitation of Mr. Sedgwick, coming over here to spend the Sunday; and as I walked along the north of the church to his residence, I was very much delighted with its external appearance, and as I passed to the centre of the street I was charmed with the view which stretched out far to the south; and the village and the church of Stratford has looked lovely in my eyes ever since. I have been absent from you more years than I was with you; and yet I am sure I can say, as I have no doubt Brother Hall can say, that we have never lost our love for this church or its members, or our pride in its inheritance. My early life was spent in Ohio, and my early student days in Oberlin, in the early days of anti-slavery excitement. And my conception of religious life and the church life was one, in which earnestness and fervor were the essential elements. I remember while in New Haven, as a member of the old Center Church, that, with a young man's pharisaism,—I suppose it must have been,—I was some little time in discovering very much piety in the Center Church; and, I suppose, had I known this church at that time, I should have been equally slow to discern the hidings of its strength. But my acquaintance with the First Church in New Haven and my acquaintance with this church, following the Western life of my boyhood, and preceding the Western pastorates, which I have had in two Western cities, have been of incalculable benefit to me. They have given me the power of appreciating, in some degree, the element of time in church life, and the element of time in the unfolding and the manifestation of personal character; and I am sure that in the historic lessons, we have been learning in the last few years, both in our church life and national life, we all of us, whether members of these historic churches or members of the newer churches of some other part of the land, are coming to appreciate, as we never did before, the conservative and preserving power of these ancient churches. There are some to-day, who question the place of the church of Christ among the forces of modern society, who call our attention to the press, to the platform, to the scientific congress and to the many influences, which are permeating and characterizing modern life. But I am sure that to-day, in this presence, and crowded and pressed as we are with the memories of the past, that we will be very slow to admit that there is anything, which God in his goodness has given this nation, which is of more value or, which has more manifest marks of his approval and affection than the gift, to this ancient church, of his Son. How many ministers, how many missionaries, how many Christian workers have gone out from the circle of churches which are to-day represented in this maternal home! I remember, when I was called upon to hear words of greeting from Brother Palmer and all the rest, the day of my ordination in this church, sixteen years ago, when our honored and beloved President Dwight preached the sermon, and when Brother Palmer gave the charge to the pastor, and Brother Davenport the right hand of fellowship, and it seems to me a very curious duty, that I should be called upon to give any words of greeting to you, for it seems but yesterday when you laid your hands on my inexperienced and untried head, and set me apart to the sacred office of pastor of this flock. But we are reminded by these changes and by these differences of relation, that we are all brethren, and that we have one common Head, even the Lord Jesus Christ. And as years and experience come to me I rejoice more and more in the work of the Christian ministry, and I trust I appreciate with some measure of earnestness and seriousness the value of these churches to this Commonwealth, and to our great Nation.

Is the problem of the hour the labor problem? Where can we find any satisfactory solution except in the gospel of our Lord Jesus Christ? Is it a question of good order among all the diversified classes of our national life? Where are we to find any fraternity, any abiding love except that which comes from the brotherhood of the Lord Jesus? Is it a question of education? The church has not only been the mother of us all but our teacher. Yale University is known in many parts of the land and the world, where these New England village churches are not known; but we come here and the historian tells us of a time, which antedated the birth of that venerable university, and the relation of these pastors and this people to the very foundation of that ancient seat of learning. And were it possible for us to trace all the influences, that have centered about that venerable seat of learning we can find that very much of it had come from the choicest life of the churches of our order in this Commonwealth. It is a National University; it is catholic toward all sects; it is hospitable toward all ideas; it is ready for any new truth; and yet the source of its inspiration and the warrant of its being was the sponsorship given by these early churches. I welcome all the churches that have been mentioned by name most heartily in the name of this mother church; and, as one by one, we see your faces and hear your voices, we will join in the universal *Te Deum* that God has given us such rich memories and such a worthy parentage, and wherever our lot may be cast we will try to be true to the churches of our order in this ancient Commonwealth.

Mr. Ives. Rev. Mr. Palmer will respond in behalf of the First Church, which has been so prolific of good in our neighboring city.

Response from the First Church, Bridgeport.

Rev. C. R. Palmer.

The relation of the First Church of Bridgeport to this ancient church in Stratford is certainly somewhat peculiar. It is not often that a child is blessed with two mothers; and yet it must be admitted that just as truly as the Stratford church is the mother of the First Church of Bridgeport, the Fairfield church is the mother of the First Church of Bridgeport. But we have this to remember that is in favor of the Stratford Church. When a movement began to set off from the Town of Stratford a few members, and from the Town of Fairfield a few members, to be incorporated as the Stratfield Parish, of which the First Church in Bridgeport is the outgrowth, our Fairfield mother was exceedingly unwilling to part with her children. The tradition is that she thought she should miss the pew taxes; and she went so far as to resist, in the General Court, a bill to incorporate the Parish of Stratfield for two or three years, and it was after four years, if I remember aright, that her opposition was overcome. Now there is no record that the Stratford mother ever showed any reluctance to have us go. Either, there were some people there as to whom she felt that their room was better than their company, or else there was a generous, liberal spirit here in Stratford, that said, "Let the children go, let them set up for themselves, we shall be all the better by-and-by because they do." Now, as there is no record that the first alternative, which I mentioned was the correct one, I incline to believe the latter was the correct one. And, standing here to represent that ancient Stratfield church, I rejoice and give thanks in the remembrance that the mother was liberal and generous enough to let us go with her blessing.

Well, sir, a good many years have passed away. Very soon we expect to celebrate the second centennial of the incorporation of that church. Things are moving fast. Perhaps, by that day, this will be the North Congregational Church of Bridgeport. If so, the mother will outrank us entirely, and we shall have to bow, whereas now we boast to be the oldest church in Bridgeport. We rejoice very much in our children, some of whom have grown to be larger than ourselves, but they all will join, I am sure, in welcoming you back to Bridgeport when you shall come.

Seriously, sir, I have a great deal of sympathy with the remarks which my Brother Fitch has made. A church of Christ in New England, with its ancient foundation and its centuries of history, is a splendid record if you can appreciate it. It is not merely what you see when you come into this town of Stratford; it is not merely what you see when you come in and look at the First Church of Bridgeport; it is not merely what you see when you come into Milford and look at the First Church of Milford, which measures the significance of one of these ancient records. Why, sir, what fountains of influence these churches have been. Four or five weeks ago I was preaching out in Central New York and when I got through and came down out of the pulpit, a lady came forward to meet me: "I want to speak to speak to you, sir," she said. "Very well, ma'am," I rejoined, "I am very happy to see you." She said, "I am a Stratford woman, and I couldn't see a Bridgeport minister in this pulpit and not want to greet him." In how many communities should we find Stratford people—why, they are scattered the country over and every where, I dare say, as in that instance, they represent the best elements of the community. So it is. Why, I have been pastor, not a great while, but long enough to remember Brother Hall here and to have taken part in Brother Fitch's installation, and Brother Dana's and Brother Ives'; and in my own church the people have scattered from it the country over till there is hardly a region in the whole nation where I can not put my finger upon some one and another and say, there is one that has gone out from this old church in Bridgeport.

Well, sir, there is a peculiar value in these ancient and long continued churches. I had to baptize a child one day in my church, and the grandfather said to me, "Well, sir, there is the beginning of the ninth generation in this church." Now, it is of value that there are communities where there are continuous lines of godly family history: of families trained in the fear of God, in the love of liberty, of righteousness and of truth. It is a proud record that this church has; it is a proud record that all these ancient New England churches have, that they have ministered to the development of the history of this nation in this indirect way of scattering children taught in the fear of God and the love of right and truth and liberty all over this broad country.

Once more, sir, as representing the First Church of Bridgeport, we hail and congratulate our Stratford mother. We rejoice in the continuance of her history to this day. We rejoice in her prosperity. This morning when we saw the cross purposes between the choir and the minister about the hymn we could not help thinking, a good deal of the independent spirit of years gone by is with her yet. Perhaps it is just as well: she will live the longer!

Mr. Ives. You remember the parable of the sheep that was lost. In hunting up our children we were delighted in happening upon a child that was lost off on the Newtown hills, and we greet her to-day.

Response from the Church in Newtown.

Rev. J. P. Hoyt.

I wish to take half a moment, of the five minutes assigned me, in relating an incident very briefly. It is said that, in a convention or gathering similar to this, the pastor of the church, in offering the introductory prayer, forgot for the moment there was more than one speaker, and so invoked the divine blessing upon the speaker of the afternoon. Then, remembering that there was another, he offered a petition for him, but, just as he was closing, he remembered that there was another still, and more to follow, and so he said in his closing words, "and may the Lord have mercy on the third speaker and those who are to follow him, and all those who are to listen to him." I cannot but think that my brother, the pastor of this church, is offering this prayer mentally, and I am very glad that I am not the nineteenth speaker, to whom you will listen after a few moments have passed.

But in regard to this lost sheep, to whom the pastor has referred, I am very glad to come to you to-day and say, the lost is found, and we are glad to be here and join in these greetings. But we deny that we were ever lost! We think the mistake is with the pastor of this church, as I can prove to you out of his own mouth, or rather, from his own pen; for, in writing to me on this subject, he said, we welcome you as a child; although, until I investigated the matter, I was in utter ignorance that we had a child upon the Newtown hills. Well, my friends, the fact is that this ancient church of Stratford is like the Queen of England in one respect, she has many daughters most happily settled in life; and there are so many of them that I suppose she sometimes forgets their names and forgets where they are and how they are. For example, there is the church in Bridgeport from whom we have just heard. She is the Princess Royal of the Royal Family, and has an empire of her own by the sea, and right grandly does she hold it and sway it.

Then there is the Woodbury church who may be compared to the Princess of Lorne, if I may use that name. She has wandered up towards Canada, far away from the mother church. But she does not dwell there 'lorn and lone, but she is in a vast Congregational berry field, Waterbury, Roxbury, Middlebury, Southbury, etc., etc. These are only specimens of the beautiful, bounteous, glorious fruits which the branches of this mother church have borne as they have run over the walls. Now, I am here to-day to represent before you the third daughter of this ancient church, who has stayed nearer the homestead and who has always been consociated with her mother and this family of churches; and we, who form this Consociation of Fairfield East, gather around our mother to day, and we ask her blessing; and all her children rise up and bless her. We are proud of our parentage; and, as we united to-day in singing the hymn, "Blest be the tie that binds," our hearts, as well as our voices, rendered blessing unto the Great Head of the church for thus binding us closely and lovingly together.

But there are some special ties which unite us to this mother church, to which I may briefly allude, though the time is so brief I can only outline them. The first tie is in the name Newtown itself. There is a tradition, (and this has become the certainty of a fact in my mind as I have investigated it,) that Newtown was called Newtown in order to distinguish her from the old town of Stratford, from which she was set off. So we are in Newtown; you are in Old-town; and all the characters which Mrs. Beecher Stowe has rendered famous and illustrious in her "Oldtown Folks" live here in Stratford without doubt. Then again, the early settlers of Newtown came from Stratford. The Hawleys who founded Hawleyville came from this place, and they gave their name to that future city. There was a family named Clark who came from this place, and one of the descendants of that family told me only this week that her ancestor, who originally came from Stratford, feeling the need of help in clearing away the wild land of Newtown, came back to Stratford; and what do you think he did? He bought a slave here in Stratford, a negro boy eight years old, paying eight pounds for him, a pound for every year of his life; carried him to Newtown, and, when there was a declaration of independence, as far as slavery was concerned, in this Commonwealth, gave him his freedom; but the noble colored brother said, "You have cared for me in my boyhood, I will care for you in your old age;" and he remained with him till the day of his death. Then there was a man by the name of Jeremiah Turner, who came from Stratford to Newtown; and it is recorded on a monument in one of the old cemeteries, that he was the father of the first male child born in Newtown. It is also recorded in the Town Records, I think, that he returned to Stratford for a wife. This Jeremiah Turner returned, so he was a *re-Turner* to the old Town of Stratford, and I venture to say that there were no "lamentatives" of that Jeremiah over his choice; and from that day to this Newtown people have been marrying Stratford people. The daughter of our senior deacon married a Stratford brother, and he is now deacon in the Newtown church. So you will see how we are tied together by these memories of the past as well as of the present.

But the most interesting use, and I allude to this in closing, Mr. Moderator, is this: that the most successful pastor the church in Newtown ever had was a native of Stratford. Rev. David Judson, born, as I have been told since I came here to-day, near the foot of your Academy Hill. He had a pastorate of one-third of a century in Newtown, and was loved where there and in all the churches of this region. He was a revolutionary soldier or chaplain, and died in the war, and his grave is with us in the Newtown cemetery to this day; and a beautiful and suggestive fact connected with it is, that, out of the very heart of the grave, there is growing an evergreen tree, keeping alive, in the memory of his successors and those who have taken up the work after him, the memory of that good and godly man, Rev. David Judson, of Stratford. With these memories in my mind, wishing I could say more, but limiting myself to this, Newtown, with her fertile farms, with her manufactures, with her four different railroads, soon to become five, with her hundreds of industrious citizens, we come back to our mother to-day, and extend to her our greetings and congratulations; and we say, giving it a meaning more true and deep and tender than the Englishmen can when they sing that song, "God save the Queen,"—the Queen mother of all these churches. And we reverently add, God save the churches themselves, and all the members of these churches, and bring us all home at last to the great family gathering in the palace of the great King.

Mr. Ives. Before singing the 1346th Hymn, I desire to say that there were no "cross purposes," as Brother Palmer suggested, but only an earnest desire on the part of the choir leader to follow out my wishes and make the services as brief as possible. We will now hear the response from the church in Huntington. Will those who are to respond from Trumbull and Monroe please come forward so as to have no delay.

RESPONSE from the Church in Huntington,

REV. A. J. PARK.

VENERABLE MOTHER: We come to you to-day with greeting, realizing how precious is this thought of coming home to our mother. The affection and love of children to mothers is that which can be realized only in the heart. It can never be told. And we come, dear mother, as a child already one hundred and sixty-five years old last February, not so very youthful, and yet vigorous and strong. In bringing you greetings it seemed to me that perhaps a bit of history of that little church away up there, that was called Ripton parish once,—now Huntington,—might be profitable. In 1724 the mother went up there and performed the nuptial vows that made a new church with a pastor who began a ministry among those hills and forty-eight years labored there alone, (in the forty-ninth year of his ministry they called an associate,) and living for three years longer, completed about fifty-two years of pastorate. Dr. Ely, who was called as an associate of Jeremiah Mills, was forty-three years there as a pastor. Unfortunately, somehow the records of Brother Mills pastorate have nearly all been lost. Only a mere sketch of the organization of the church is to be found; no record of the number of members that were added to the church during his ministry, nor those that were baptized. From the time that Dr. Ely came into the church, the records appear very correctly, and we have received from that time, with those who were at the organization of the church, something over three hundred and thirty, making an average of five and a-half annually gathered into the church. Dr. Ely, when he became pastor, adopted the special part of the Covenant which reads as follows: "That you will endeavor by the strength of God to walk in all his commandments and ordinances blameless, desiring to put yourselves under the watch and care of this church, to be trained up in the school of Christ for His Heavenly Kingdom, promising also that you will give up your children to God in baptism and to bring them up in the fear of the Lord." A little part of that I have never seen in any Covenant before. As a result of this you may see in the records of Dr. Ely, baptized in the church in forty-three years, eight hundred and fifty-seven, a yearly average of twenty; thus bringing before us a thought that it seems to me we need to go back to, realizing our Covenant relationship with God, realizing our obligation as Christian parents to our children, inheritors with us of the blessings and privileges of the gospel. This part of the Covenant seems to have been left out at the end of his ministry, but during the next twenty-eight years the yearly average was six and a-seventh, and during the last forty-five years only two and a-half. So we see how the gradual diminishing of the thought of this covenant relation of parents with their children has grown up among the people. The largest membership of the church was in the year 1833, when the number reached two hundred and three. During the last forty-five years there have been ten preachers. I believe only two of them have been installed, their time of labor ranging from a year and a-half to six years and a-half, so you see while the time has been about equal to that of Dr. Ely, ten ministers have occupied the pulpit, and the results have been only partially what they were during his, in regard to the receiving and baptizing of children, and, also, to the membership of the church.

Now, as we have only this moment, let us pray that God will bless and prosper, not only the mother but the children in all that which tends to build up and to establish the faith of the saints. Praying that God may bless and cheer and comfort you in this your age, we greet you with our richest blessing.

Mr. Ives. Mr. H. L. Fairchild for the church in Unity.

Response from the Church in Trumbull.

H. L. Fairchild.

Mr. Mother: I would be glad to be consigned in accordance with your mother goose insinuation, but our church has grown altogether too old for any such consignment. To your kindly greetings and hearty welcome we respond to-day with the heartiest thanks; and it seems, as we come before you on such a memorable family gathering, that it is entirely proper that the daughter should tell some of her experiences; and I was reminded by your suggestion in regard to the main chance at the dinner of an incident which occurred a few years before our church was organized, at about the time of the early settlement. Then there was a great snow. Cotton Mather tells us of it in his "Magnalia." It was about the year 1717, and, if the accounts are at all correct, it completely distances the blizzard of a year and a-half ago. The people in Stratford became solicitous in regard to the stock of provision in the outlying settlements; so a party went out, dug their way through up into our region, and found a house very nearly covered with snow, the chimney barely peeping out. They found their way inside, and, instead of a shortness, the people there were just sitting down to a dinner of roast wild turkey, and they with great benevolence joined the circle and helped demolish the turkey. I think, Mr. Mother, that we have to-day paid off the score, if not before!

Our first minister, the Rev. Richardson Minor, settled, as you see, in 1730, was a man of ceremonious, formal, methodical habits, and, as might naturally be expected, after a successful ministry of fourteen years, he joined the more prosperous ministry of the Episcopal church, and, in doing so, you have referred to his giving you much trouble. He gave us still more, for our church was practically demoralized and disheartened, and it took us four years more to recuperate and start again. Then followed the ministry of Rev. James Beebe, a man in singular contrast to his pedecessor, being active, vigorous, and independent. His independence, perhaps, was shown in his treatment of church counsels; for, while he was warm-hearted in his fellowship with all the neighboring churches, he would brook nothing like authority. His own church was independent in that respect. His courage was manifest during the French war, for, after several seasons of disheartening disaster, he aroused his people and enlisted them for the war, and went with them himself in the succesful campaign which permanently checked the French power. Likewise again, in the darkest days of the Revolution, he went with the army for six months at Valley Forge; and perhaps in nothing was his independence more clearly shown than in his complete disdain of English orthography, for in looking over his record in his marching list may be found on a single page the word "March" spelled in eight different ways. His pastorate lasted for thirty-eight years. The next longest pastorate is that of the Rev. N. T. Merwin, about twenty-five years, too recent for me to speak of, further than to say his evident aim was to live "Wise as a serpent and harmless as a dove." These three pastorates cover very nearly half of our life as a church.

We have had many good deacons of the genuine New England sort, one of whom said one day to a neighbor that he considered his office worth to him, in the way of business, $50 a year. It is also said of one of our deacons that he held the office for over fifty years, and was present at every communion, and during all the years of his active service only failed once to officiate. On that occasion, on his way to the meeting, on horseback, he was thrown from his horse and broke his collar-bone. He sat through the morning service, and then was obliged to retire to have the bone adjusted. An aged St. Louis lady, long since dead, told me the story; and, although sainted, I am almost afraid to call her aged! Another widow, almost ninety years of age, among us, was one day asked by a younger relative how old she was. "A very improper question," was the reply, "under the circumstances a very improper question, indeed." A good Christian and charitable brother among us one Fast Day morning was approached by a neighbor pleading illness, and he sold him a glass of spirits. That day, on his way to meeting, he found the young men and boys playing the national game of ball on the Green. In holy indignation he remonstrated, but in vain. Then he proceeded to take down their names for prosecution, but, being reminded of the sale of cider in the morning, he saw the situation, and so charitably forebore to prosecute!

We have through all these years fairly maintained our

strength, although our town has increased but little in population, and although many other churches have come in; yet our numbers are to-day greater than at any time in our past history; and we come here joyfully to congratulate you on your illustrious history of two hundred and fifty years. We congratulate you on the number of colonies which you have sent out as churches to be influences for good. We congratulate you on the individuals who have gone out from you to almost every part of the world to maintain the standard of right, and we especially congratulate you for the tide which is rolling in upon you from the west, which, like a new element to reinvigorate, is like the notorious elixir; for we believe, with others that have spoken here to-day, that a church has no right to grow old, much less to die, so long as there are souls to save; and the best wish that we can extend to you to-day is that responsibility may so come in upon you that by exercise you shall maintain a manly, useful strength, a radiant, maidenly, Christian loveliness, to win souls to Christ.

Mr. Ives. You will next hear from New Stratford, Deacon W. Well Lewis. I hope Deacon Lewis will take the platform, otherwise it is almost impossible for those in the galleries to hear. It is of no use to speak if you cannot make yourself heard.

Response from the Church in Monroe,

Deacon W. Wells Lewis.

It would be very natural for any person in this house, after hearing such kindly words of welcome, after listening to so many words of greeting, and after hearing so much that is calculated to benefit and instruct, to be able to say something. I am here to-day, and the thought that suggested itself to me as I came down here was: "I am coming home, coming home." Now, the sound of my voice never before was heard within these walls, yet I am one of your number, I am one of your household, I am one of your family. I am here to-day to hold out to you friendly greetings. I am here to-day to enter into your sympathies. I am here to-day to be one among you.

A long period of years ago, this church put forth its branches, and many branches of righteousness have grown up and become transplanted in the heavenly Jerusalem above. The thought suggested itself to me: Suppose that all the members of this household, suppose that all this company should be gathered together and should rise up to you to-day, how large a church would we need in order to accommodate you? A very large structure would certainly be needed. In the little town of Monroe our church is not large, our members are few: yet we have those there, that are praying men. We have praying men, praying women. There are those there who live daily in the atmosphere of a Saviour's love. There are those who live in constant, daily communion with their God. They are fully satisfied that in order to reach Christian manhood and womanhood they have got to seek for it, they have got to work for it. We have an active minister, a minister that is not satisfied with theory alone, but theory and practice must go hand in hand. I am exceedingly sorry that he could not be here to-day to respond to this call. We have in the little town of Monroe a Society of Christian Endeavor which is doing a mighty work. It is doing a powerful work, more perhaps than any other young people's organization we have ever had there. Taking it altogether, although our numbers are few, we say in the language of David, "If God be for us who can be against us?" And now, this gathering here to-day is a joyous one, it is a glorious one, it is one that will be remembered a long time. Will it not, my brethren, be remembered till that glorious gathering when all these grandchildren, when all these great-grandchildren, when all these sons and daughters, that have grown up as the branches of the spiritual vine shall stand up triumphant together in the streets of the New Jerusalem? I am here to-day to hold out to you the right-hand of Christian fellowship. I am here to mingle my voice with your voices, and also to receive the benediction of the mother. Finally, friends, when this mighty work shall be accomplished; when we shall go away, as we soon shall to our homes, we shall separate one from another, and we shall have formed acquaintances here that will never be forgotten; and when we come to meet each other this gathering will be spoken of. Reminiscences will be brought up. The kindly feelings entertained here, the new acquaintances that we have formed here, will be held up there; but this will not be the end of it. Eternity, Eternity itself will only disclose the glorious reality of this home gathering.

Singing, Hymn written for the occasion, by the pastor. [See page 11.]

MR. IVES. We will now hear a response from the church in Southbury by the Rev. David C. Pierce.

RESPONSE from the Church in Southbury.

REV. DAVID C. PIERCE.

THE grandchild of Southbury cordially responds to your kind greeting; and we will say that, although you have traces of antiquity about you, we would scarcely know it, and we rejoice that there is no decadence in strength. We rejoice to be with you and all the children and grandchildren that have gathered together here upon this happy occasion; and although we stand here before you representing a grandchild of this ancient church, yet we feel that in a certain sense we also have a little of antiquity about us. It is about one hundred and fifty-seven years since the church was first started to preach the Word of God in Southbury. Branching off from the First Church of Woodbury, they erected a church in the beautiful valley of Pomperaug, and we feel particularly proud that we may say that the first pastor of that church, the Rev. John Graham, was a descendant of the Marquis of Montrose, who labored there some thirty-three years, and was a most efficient and worthy laborer in the Church of Christ. To show you some of the disadvantages, when we started, although they began service immediately after he was settled, yet it was some three years before the church was finished, and for those three years, during the greater portion of the time, they worshipped with only a part of a floor laid; the windows were not in place and a large portion of the building unplastered. At that time they had no means of warming the church except such little means as were provided by foot-stoves, the ladies brought to church. Now, we should think it hard, indeed, to worship among the inclemency of our New England winters in the structures of those times and have no better warmth than one fireplace. The Rev. John Graham lived there until feebleness and sickness coming on, put a close to his labors, but he remained some eight years longer till he died. His remains now rest in the North Cemetery in our village. After him came Benjamin Wildman, who labored some forty-seven years in that church, a man noted for his wit and the aptness of his replies. It was during his ministry, in the year 1772, that the second church was erected. The first building was used as a place of worship some forty years. After him came a succession of laborers in the field, among them the Rev. Elias Wood, who labored some three years, who was followed by the Rev. Daniel Clark, who labored three years longer; and during the next seven years there was no settled minister, but they were supplied by three or four laborers in the service. After this came the Rev. Thomas Shipman, father of Judge Shipman, who was with them ten years, and was a most efficient laborer, and during the period of his ministry there was a large revival and many were received into the church. There was one item I forgot to mention when I was speaking of the first minister, the Rev. John Graham, showing the efficiency of his labors, that during the period of his ministry over three hundred members were received into the church, and over eight hundred children were baptized. Thus we feel that we can show a record concerning the former laborers in this branch of the Lord's heritage that shows that we had earnest men in the days of old; and although we, like our grandmother, show something of the signs of decadence, as you know that many of the New England villages are not in a flourishing condition, but population is being drawn off toward the centers of trade and commerce; yet we trust we have something of the spirit of God in us, and we can cordially respond to the greeting upon this occasion and desire that all the children and grandchildren who are represented here to-day may unite together,

with this ancient church, in ascribing praise unto God who
hath wrought thus far in his work amongst us, and that we
may be counted as worthy laborers as well as the fathers of
old, in carrying forward this good work: and with that view
in mind the church which I represent sends to you this sentiment: In memory of our venerable forefathers who were so
earnest in the cause of God: May we imitate their virtues and
may we strive to follow in their footsteps, ever bearing in mind,
their memory with tender emotions.

MR. IVES. We will now hear from Dr. Bellamy on the hills
of Bethlehem by the mouth of the beloved John—my class-
mate, the Rev. John P. Trowbridge.

RESPONSE from the Church in Bethlehem,

REV. J. P. TROWBRIDGE.

BELOVED BROTHER: Fifteen years ago last Spring we went
out together from our studies in a Theological Seminary, and
now, to-day, we meet, you to represent an aged and superb
grandmother, and I to represent a curly-headed grandchild.
And in meeting thus together upon this happy commemorative
occasion, our minds have of course those feelings natural to
class-mates who sojourned together and studied together for
three years, natural to those who at the same time or nearly
at the same time began the Christian ministry, natural to those
who have in the work of the Christian ministry been endeavor-
ing to present the truth as it is in Christ. Many of you remember that Mr. Longfellow, near the close of his life, when
he was called upon to participate in exercises of deep interest
to himself and to the college of which he was a graduate, began, that beautiful poem, one of the most beautiful of all
his writings, by citing the custom of the Roman Gladiator,
saying, "We, who are about to die, salute you." And I have
thought, as I have anticipated this pleasant meeting with the
ancient church of Stratford, that if in those ancient days of
Rome, amid the pageants and surroundings where they were
placed, they could look up at their great rulers and say, as they
were about to enter into a contest like that which we are enter-

ing into, against principalities and powers in the high places of the earth, "We, who are about to die, salute you," certainly their brethren and friends in the Christian ministry, we who have not died, we who are representatives of the ancient church of New England, who cannot expect to die, may certainly with great gratitude and joy salute this ancient church, its pastor, its membership, it daughters and its granddaughters. We come here to-day, amid these favorable influences and bright surroundings. We greet one another as a common family. Our names are all on a common line, none of them being elevated above the other, all standing together in a common place representing upon a common platform the unity and the brotherhood that we enjoy. We are grateful for the memories of the past, grateful for the truth that has been proclaimed, as it has been represented in the discourse this morning from the ministry of this ancient church, to uphold the gospel in its purity and power. Every one of these churches has pecular memories. The church in Bethlehem has a peculiar tribute of gratitude to bring to lay upon the altar here of her grandmother's affection and household care. Turn back to the early history of the church in the east part of the north purchase, now called Woodbury, and you find that Dr. Bellamy was licensed to preach the gospel when, I think, he was eighteen years of age, in the year 1736, by the Fairfield East Association of ministers, with which the pastors of this church, I doubt not, have been generally associated, and in 1754, when great events in the life of Dr. Bellamy occurred, and he was so earnestly called to go to the First Presbyterian Church in New York and there labor and spend the most fruitful years of his life, he laid the matter, that was so weighty upon his mind, that he could not decide at first, before the Consociation of Litchfield County; and after they had deliberated sufficiently in regard to it, not being able to come to a decision, they called to their fellowship, and for mutual consideration, the Fairfield East Consociation, with which this church has been connected. So you see, friends, that his early Christian life work was at Bethlehem, where the best years of his life were spent, and where it is a providence of God that he was permitted to live, for if he had gone to New York, whence he was called with such earnestness, at the time he was called, and had spent in that metropolis the best years of his life, during the confusion of the Revolutionary War it is very doubtful, if he ever would have given to the church of New England the body of divinity that he composed, and have exerted the influence he did as a theological teacher in the early history of New England. So I do not exceed the bounds of the truth and the proper expression of it when I say we are deeply obligated, not simply in Bethlehem, but all the churches of Connecticut, for the influences that the church of Stratford and the consociated churches in the Fairfield East Consociation exerted upon the mind of Dr. Bellamy, that kept him within our limits; and that enabled him to live and devote his time to that work that has made him pre-eminent in our Commonwealth as a writer, as a theological thinker, as a teacher in the chair of Theology. I bless God to-day that I am permitted to bring to you the congratulations of the church of which he was the first minister, over which for fifty years he was the faithful pastor, and from which his spirit speaks to-day.

Mr. IVES. You will listen now to the greeting from the church in Washington, another granddaughter, by Deacon E. W. Woodruff.

RESPONSE from the Church in Washington,

DEACON E. W. WOODRUFF.

WELL, Grandmother, I bring to you Mr. Turner's best and sincere regrets that he cannot be here to-day to greet you, therefore I come in his place. You will not let me tell what we have done up there, I can't with that five minute sword hanging over my head; but I will tell you what we have got, and I bet you can't guess. What do you guess? We have got a Swedish baby. It was born the first Sacramental season in May, 1889. The way of it is this. Up in our farming country towns, years ago and now, all the brightest and best boys and girls go off to the city and out West, where they can get knowledge and make money a great deal better than they can here, and leave us poor sticks at home; and what is father and mother to do? They had before called in Pat and Bridget, from the land of the Celt, but we up there in Judea think we know a thing or two, and we called in Gustavus and Lena from the land of the Swedes. The Swedes brought the Bible with them and wanted to worship God in their own language. They had their minister come; they built a hall, or started to build one: and we chipped in and helped them. They wanted to form a church. Well, Yankee ingenuity came in and we said, here, suppose you come and join our church, meet down in the hall and worship in your own language; but you shall belong to our church and be a branch. Very well, so on that Sabbath there were over thirty that joined our church. Our articles of faith and covenant were translated into Swedish and the Swedish minister read them to the communicants and the communion service was administered in both Swedish and English. Well, now, what was all this for? These Swedish children come to our church, come to our school. But this is only temporary, remember, and soon the clannish Swede will be supplanted with the millennial English. And when you sent us up into the hills, full of Yankee sagacity, of foresight and hindsight, we were looking ahead. Up in these New England hills, Congregational churches are, many of them, reduced so low they are not able to starve one man, but have to do it two together, to do it decently, to starve one minister! We do not expect any such thing is going to arrive there. Our little baby is growing very fast. There is about fifty of her now. The last communion season there was about fifteen more of her admitted. You see the point. We have city people there to be sure, but they come and go. Blessings on them while they stay! But then comes the cold Winter,—what are you going to do? We don't want to go into holes like woodchucks and hibernate: and as we get old and totter by the fireplace, in comes this buxom Swedish lass and makes things sweet, and, God bless her, she is a source of help and comfort to us. This we call "the Judea patent process of preserving the churches." In three years more we shall be one hundred and fifty years old. Well, may I say one word or two! We have done something up on that old hill. We have had some high old fights in the abolition times and temperance times, plenty of them; but we had good old "Stratford grit," and we always won in the end. We raised a school teacher there, who was a Gunn, and he shot new ideas into the system of education; and he was one of the first to learn men how to train that animal, the crudest curiosity on God's earth, a boy, through what Henry Ward Beecher said was the "Hell gate" he had to pass through, twelve to sixteen years old. He who had set forward progress in that line of education lies buried on our hill. We say that a church and town are one in New England, and you cannot separate them, that is impossible. We sent our Senator Platt who lived there until after his majority, and who worthily represents us in the halls of Congress—but I must not linger—only we wish you would come up and see us. If you will come up and make us a real good visit this Fall, some day, we will give you plenty of pumpkin pies and apple sauce; and if you will bring your cap and stay over Sunday we will let you go down and see the baby. Well, I am delegated to give to you our Christian greeting, our heartiest Christian greeting and congratulations, and happy to find you in such a green old age. And we pray that you may live, not only through a green old age, but a thousand years, and not only a thousand years, but to the time when the apocalyptic angel shall stand with one foot on sea and one on land and declare that time shall be no more.

Mr. Ives. I am reminded by this that we ought perhaps to have included another church, that we could have put in the place of that blank panel, our Scandinavian Church in Bridgeport, and if there has been any oversight in this regard I will make free acknowledgment at this time.

Is there any one present to represent the church in Roxbury? No name has been given to us. I will take but a moment to say, that during my first year in the Seminary I was sent up to Roxbury to preach. It was my first output from the Seminary. I took with me the only two sermons I owned, and I preached them and came home!

We will now listen to a response from the church in South Britain by Brother John Pierce.

RESPONSE from the Church in South Britain.

MR. JOHN PIERCE.

IN behalf of the great-great-grandchildren of South Britain we are here to thank you for the courtesy and kindness extended to us. I might say South Britain is a little village situated in the extreme northwest corner of New Haven county, bounded on the west by the ancient Pootatuck, or present Housatonic river. Our ancestors came from this neighborhood and the adjoining town of Milford, up the valley of the Housatonic, thence to the valley of the Pomperaug and Shepaug, into the town of Woodbury, and then returned southerly in this direction, forming the town of Southbury, and latterly the parish of South Britain, a portion of the town of Southbury. Our church, as you will see, was organized in the year 1763, splitting off from the church in Southbury, representing, that the high hills between were such an impediment that it was difficult for them to attend that church. They petitioned the General Assembly for a site, and after some debate and opposition they were organized into a church by themselves. The name of the place, as near as can be ascertained, was originated in this way: South, lying south of Woodbury; and Britain, because the inhabitants were loyal subjects to the English Crown, a fact which caused them great inconvenience during the war of the Revolution. Perhaps it is not well to say this, but facts are facts. A portion of my ancestors came from this direction, the town of Wethersfield and Glastonbury. Our early ancestors were most anxious to form a church. They were anxious to serve their Maker according to the best of their abilities. In order to show you the rigidness with which they wished God's commands to be obeyed, I will read to you a writ that has been in the possession of my family ever since its original draft, issued for Sabbath breaking:

"To John Pierce, Esq., Justice of the Peace for Litchfield "County, comes David Pierce and Robert Edmonds, Grand

"Jurymen for our Lord the King in said County, and by reason
" of their office, oath, complaint and presentment make of and
" against Stephen Squire, of Woodbury, with County aforesaid,
" for that he the said Stephen Squires did on the 9th of May,
" A. D. 1773, being Sabbath or Lord's day, he the said Stephen
" being in good health refused and neglected to attend on any
" publick worship in any meeting or congregation in said Town
" or elsewhere, but did wilfully Absent himself therefrom by
" gayly staying at home Without any work of Necessity or
" Mercy Obliging him thereto which is contrary to our statute
" law of the Colony Entitled an act for the due observance and
" keeping of the Sabbath or Lord's day, and to the bad Exam-
" ple of his Majestie's good Subjects, and prays a writ of our
" Lord, the King, may go forth against the said Stephen and
" he be dealt with as the law directs.
" Dated at Woodbury the 19th day of May, A. D. 1773.
" David Pierce,   Robert Edmond,
" Grand Jury-Men."

I have good evidence that the said Stephen was prosecuted as the law directed and punished for the offense. The idea seemed to be in those days that a church could be supported after the people had acquired a certain amount of wealth. The Society of South Britain represented to the General Court that they had a taxable property amounting to one thousand, two hundred pounds; and the first minister, Jehu Miner, was awarded a settlement of two hundred pounds, and an annual salary of seventy pounds a year. This was a very nice thing for a young clergyman, who had possibly spent the larger part of his money in getting his education; and the idea of taxing the society fell with us into innocuous desuetude about the year 1830. About the year 1803, when a tax was laid upon the society contrary to the wishes of many, an old farmer turned out to the tax collector a large black bear which he had brought from Minnesinks, New York State, with his Bible; the bear and Bible were sold at the post, and the money used to pay the society tax. That is a fact.

The next minister after Jehu Miner was Rev. Matthew

Cazier, a man of French extraction, of strong Calvinistic principles. It was said, I don't know how true it is, that he used to chastise his son almost every day in the week for fear that he might disregard the text, "He that spares the rod will spoil the child."

The next minister of eminence was the Rev. Bennett Tyler whom many of you brethren will remember, who attained great eminence in his profession, one of the greatest theologians of the State in his day and time. Of the fourteen ministers who have officiated in our parish, I believe all have been men of God, and all have striven sincerely and earnestly to worship Him and lead their flocks according to the best of their ability.

CHURCH DECORATIONS. (LOOKING EAST.)

Mr. IVES. We will now hear a response from the North Church of Woodbury, by the Rev. Mr. Wyckoff.

Response from the North Church of Woodbury,

REV. J. L. R. WYCKOFF.

I REPRESENT, SIR, the third generation of a race of ministers, and I can remember, when a child in my mother's home, many gatherings of ministers around the table, and I have a very distinct recollection of being compelled to wait when the ministers were visiting at our home; and my chief anxiety was, when they were eating, whether anything would be left when they got through, for you know those religious eaters. We had the evidence of that to-day; and I confess it was a matter of considerable anxiety to me, while sitting in the pew over there, whether or not there would be anything left when those who preceded me got through in the way of refreshment this afternoon.

I see that I am not recognized here in this home, and it may be necessary for me to make a word of explanation. The thing to do here to-day is in some way or another to connect yourself with Stratford. I have wondered how I could do it. My grandfather was a Presbyterian minister of the old school. My father was a Presbyterian minister of the new school. They left me on the fence. I jumped down between, and the good people of North Woodbury, seeing I was a stranger, took me in. They took me in, for when they had once received me, they administered to me this oath: No man shall preach the gospel in this church except the man who preaches the pure doctrines of the gospel commonly known as Calvanistic, or as contained in the Shorter Catechism of the Westminster Assembly. I said they took me in—with my consent, of course. I want to say in regard to your grandchild to-day, the first thing and the most important thing in regard to her church life, she has held fast to the faith once delivered to the saints. It is the first time that I have ever been privileged to look into the face of Grandmother Stratford. I wonder, if she had the faith to deliver to-day, if she would deliver it as unalloyed, as in those days,—as pure and simple. The time came when the little swallow had to be crowded off the eaves, and she flew away and found herself a nest, a very pleasant one and commodious, capable of accommodating from five to seven hundred little nestlings. She has pushed on in the presence of misfortune until to-day she outnumbers on her list her mother, in the way of communicants; and she has pushed up until she reaches almost your own record of church membership, seventy-three years of church life, seventy-three years of faithful witnessing to the truth and holding fast to the faith as it is Jesus. It is a pleasant thing for us to come back to-day, and make a report as to the way in which we have served the Master and held to the faith. It is a great thing to be put into the line of spiritual descent, to have the hand of a pious ancestor extended with benediction over one's life. Descent is important, but ascent is better. We thank God for what has been transmitted to us, for the prayers that have been answered with respect to our church life, and for the sympathy that has been extended to us, although we have not seen your face for all these seventy-three years. It seems a little strange that we should come here to-day and protest our affection, when we have never as yet exchanged a visit; but it seems equally strange that this our grandmother should be so ignorant with reference to our name. I presume there is not a member of my church who would recognize the name on that panel, not one, Woodbury Second. It is North Woodbury, and, just as the brother has intimated, these inscriptions are all on the same level. We don't recognize either first or second. It is Woodbury South, or South Woodbury, and Woodbury North, or North Woodbury. The saints are one, as they have one faith, one Lord, one baptism.

It will not do for me to trespass on this brother's patience. I heard him say over in the aisle, unless I misunderstood him, to Brother Hovey, "The man who exceeds five minutes will be imprisoned." I want to keep my liberty. I was born free, and I want to preserve it. I will simply close by saying to you that all the saints in North Woodbury greet you, and request me to salute you with a holy kiss; and they unite with me in the most earnest and fervent prayer that God may bless you and keep you and cause his face to shine upon you and be gracious unto you.

Mr. Ives. We are now getting down toward the children of a younger growth, and the Rev. R. G. S. McNeille, will respond for the Second Church in Bridgeport.

RESPONSE from the South Church in Bridgeport,

REV. R. G. S. McNEILLE.

MR. MODERATOR AND BRETHREN OF THE STRATFORD CHURCH: When Father Tom Burke, the Priest, was pleading in England the cause of Ireland, he laid great emphasis, in connection with his eloquent appeals, upon the fact that he himself was an Irishman. The next day the English Historian, Mr. Froude, in a public address, called Father Tom to account and said he ought not to boast of being an Irishman, because the name Burke was a Norman name. But Father Tom, upon a subsequent occasion, said that Mr. Froude had claimed that Burke was a Norman name, and, said he, Mr. Froude is correct, although the name has rested upon the old sod for four hundred years; but, perhaps, Mr. Froude does not know that my mother was a Callihan, though everybody knows that Callihan is an Irish name, and that the boys take after their mother. As I have met here so pleasantly the representatives of these churches in these felicitously arranged exercises, I congratulate you, first of all, that the descendants of this ancient and honored church follow the general rule and alike take after their mother. They are marked with the imprint of her face. They still hold, the very faith received through her at the first; not the faith of the Westminster Catechism, however excellent: not the faith of John Calvin, however profound; not the faith of John Wesley, however stimulating; these influences, fall into the second place, but the one faith of the Lord Jesus Christ, our Lord and our Redeemer, held under whatever system of doctrine and under whatever subordinate human name you please, the faith that makes our hearts glow and brings us into love and sympathy with his divine way of life, of glory and of salvation.

Meanwhile, I do not forget to express a deep sympathy with the idea that has been so often averted to here, the value in church life of historical continuity, and I am glad now at length to attend a celebration of one of the original Puritan Churches, which commemorates in to-day's anniversary an appreciable portion of a millennial of history. And while it is true that we who are Congregational claim, even from the earliest Church in Jerusalem, a continuity of principle in regard to faith and practice; yet in these last days, it is felicitous for us to feel that here we are gaining in respect of that outward continuity, which is historically associated with common institutions long preserved and handed down. I feel now, at length, that our Congregationalism begins to assume the type of some of those great European cathedrals, dating back in the origin of their continuous growth and erection to earlier centuries, but added to in every succeeding century by the contributions of an ever fresh, an ever growing and an ever potent piety. I greet you, therefore, first of all from our church, because we have so much in common, we have our histories in common; we have our Christian life from a common source and we have in common the spirit which energizes a pure New Testament faith. I think that we of the Second Church in Bridgeport rejoice also that we may bring you greetings because of the perpetuity of the Union of those Churches—a union in organization, and in fellowship—which has arisen from these old centers of New England life and theology. I remember that on one occasion a youthful student in the Seminary spoke to the Rev. Dr. Bacon of the Congregational Churches as being a rope of sand. "Yes," said Dr. Bacon, "you see the sand, I see the rope." And I have often thought that our Churches are as jewels prepared for a crown, separate in their integrity, in their beauty and in their individual value, but joined together as some of the royal jewels are often joined, by a filligree of gold almost invisible, a true and golden bond so that the joints do not appear. I congratulate you, therefore, upon the unity of our Churches, a unity which, however slight it may seem, is sufficiently strong, as seen to-day, for sympathy and work during the two hundred and fifty years which are past and gone.

I congratulate you, last of all, on the continued individuality of the Churches. I am glad to hear from such a one, as the brother who preceeded me, his staunch allegiance and the staunch allegiance of his Church to an ancient and noble creed. I am glad to hear from all of our Churches concerning that which, while they are Congregational and united, makes them individual also in the freedom of their growth, in the activity of their life in the pursuit of a common purpose. Each Church values for itself differing forms of thought and we emphasize, somewhat varying theologies, but, nevertheless, individual in our freedom, we do no more than give, as it were, a varied expression to our invaluable and holy Christian faith. I feel that, in regard to our unity, we are to-day, as ever, one. I feel that in regard to our individuality we are to-day, as ever, many, in order that, if any one Church may be able to contribute or preserve any specially valuable thought or practice all the rest are at liberty to receive that contribution, and thankfully using it may at length make it common to us all. Just as in some cathedrals you see the great rose-window which in the west of the church takes up and transmits the light of a perfect day, and when you look at it and look out through it you see the amber and the gold and the royal purple and the amethyst, the shining blue, and the deep ruby,—all these colors perfect in their adjustment,—the perfect picture according to the artist's mind, yet if you turn your back to that window and look toward the altar, you will find that through these many single pieces of stained glass, all of them of different colors, there comes from the whole window, upon the altar of God's house a pure white and combined light. So I congratulate you, that from this ancient church so many churches have arisen, individual in their planting, and individual in their free growth but that through them all, taken together, there still shines the white light of the Gospel of redeeming love. And if there should fall upon some of the young men and upon some of the young women of this church that spirit of prophecy that was spoken of by an elder Prophet of by-gone days; if it were given to any here in that spirit of prophecy to look ahead for two hundred and fifty years, I can express no better wish than that catching the light from the mountain top of Zion, across so many sunken and hidden valleys of the unrevealed future, the spirit of prophecy might discern afar off, that when another quarter millennial shall have been completed, and when history shall have swelled the stream of our church life to twice its present magnitude and bulk, that even in that far off time, this ancient and Godly church may still be able to gather around her, her children and her children's children, consecrated to one faith, one Lord, one baptism of the Holy Ghost; to a common penitence and a common hope of everlasting salvation.

COLLECTION OF RELICS AT LECTURE ROOM.

Mr. Ives. Dr. Hovey will now respond for the Park Street Church. Will the other gentlemen please come forward.

Response from the Park Street Church, Bridgeport.

Rev. H. C. Hovey, D.D.

My Dear Brother: I received from you a postal card closing with the touching words, "Remember the Belle." Thus the Pastor of this church speaks of the dear old grandmother. She is the belle whom we all love, beautiful as in the days of her youth. Far away on the banks of the Muscoka, north of the Georgian Bay last Sunday morning, I met with a group of Christian people to worship God, and one of them said to me, you are going to have a celebration at Stratford, we understand this coming week. Dear old Stratford! At New York, in one of the busiest offices on Broadway I met one of the busiest men of all in that great throbbing metropolis, and as we parted, after transacting a little business, he said, there is going to be a great celebration down at Stratford next Thursday. And so we hear from one and another of those who love your belle. Away off in Minneapolis, when a dear brother had expounded the Scriptures to us in such a manner as to make them luminous, and I asked him where he came from, he said he came from dear old Stratford. I am glad to see him here to-day, your former Sunday-School superintendent, Brother Plant. Thus we all are here with our tribute of love to the belle; and perhaps after all, deciphering your hieroglyphics which I do with joy and pleasure, my brother, I may have misunderstood the matter, and it may be the young church of which I am the pastor that you wish me to speak of. Remember the Belle! How could I forget that beautiful young church of only twenty years, strong, lithe, ruddy in her youth and beauty. May God bless her, your grandchild, the Park Street Church, with its four hundred and fifty members, its Sunday-School averaging four hundred, take the year around, its Society of Christian Endeavor so full of life and spirits, its Mother's Meeting so goodly and strong,—all its beautiful features, I trace back through its parents to its grandmother. I say its parents; for we have not been able to decide yet whether we were born of the First Church or the Second Church, both claiming us, and we loving both and cherishing them dearly in our hearts. We know who our grandmother is!

But after all I am not sure about the postal card. There is no "e" at the end of the word belle, so it must be that you have reference to the bell that swings and summons to the house of worship; and it may be that in your pride you spoke of that old bell that used to sound down in Sandy Hollow, when all around through Connecticut the Puritans were blowing their horns to come to the House of God, or were sounding their conch shells, or, as in East Haven, good old Deacon

Austin in his regimentals was marching up and down the hill beating his big base drum in order to gather men to the House of God. Then you, in those days were swinging the first bell of goodly Connecticut. Yes, remember the bell, don't forget that. I saw the tongue of the bell, the iron tongue that cracked the old bell, not that bell, perhaps; but some other bell, it is there in the hall of relics—I am not sure I am pointing in the right direction, but you know what I mean—but I saw it. Oh how many times that bell has summoned men to worship God, how many times it has rebuked the profane Sabbath breaker; how many times it has tolled the knell for those, who have passed away from earth to heaven. Yes, remember the bell, and cherish it, for it is God's voice, it is the voice of God's bride sounding abroad through the land, rebuking the careless, summoning the thoughtful, encouraging those who are ready to repair to the House of God and to enter into his service gladly. Yes, there is one thing that we can boast of in the Park Street Church, and I don't know of any other church that can, we hear the ringing of this bell. Perhaps you can hear ours, as the bells peal on the Sabbath morning, calling men to the House of Prayer. Oh, I love the church going bell and I think of all the bells that have been set chiming and still chime to the glory of God. And that first old bell at Sandy Hollow, I say let us remember the bell. I don't know how big that bell was. We don't believe in very big bells in our Congregational churches. In the Cathedral at Montreal they have a bell that weighs 29,400 pounds. That is a monstrous bell, and over in China I have been told that the largest bell there is inscribed with 100,000 characters, and every one of those characters is a prayer, and when the bell is rung all those prayers are supposed to arise to Heaven. And now, my brethren and sisters in this old Stratford church, if we had over there at the Park Street Church a tower like the tower of Eiffel and we had swinging in this belfry such a bell as that in the Cathedral of Montreal, and if it were inscribed with a hundred thousand or a million characters, and every one a prayer, when the bell rings those prayers should arise to God for you and your church. May God bless you.

Mr. IVES. We will now hear a response from J. J. Rose, Esq., for the Olivet Church.

RESPONSE from the Olivet Church, Bridgeport.

J. J. ROSE, ESQ.

MR. GRANDMOTHER: It is not my intention to find a great deal of fault, but I do wish to say one thing in that direction. We grandchildren have had a delightful time here to-day. We have had a jolly good time. We have enjoyed every minute of it. But we do not like to come here and be told we are going to hear five minute speeches, and then hear orations of fifteen minutes. We object to that, Mr. Grandmother, and therefore, to make up for it, I had made up my mind that I would deliver an oration of an hour and a half; finally I thought that I should inflict just as much suffering upon myself as upon the rest of the children; so I have concluded to ask you that in our next two hundred and fiftieth re-union you will let us grandchildren speak first. I have no doubt though, in my heart, that you are to-day delighting in these richly dressed children of yours; but, you know, in family re-unions there are another kind of children, as well as the rich and distinguished. We find in church re-unions and family re-unions rich relations and poor relations. I come here representing one of the poor relations.

Mr. Grandmother, Olivet Church, your grandchild, learned for the first time, to my knowledge, when you sent the invitation, that she was a grandchild; so we held a jollification meeting at once. We threw up our hats to think that we were of such a distinguished line of ancestry; and I began to look back in memory upon our church record during our existance of twenty years, and I called to mind that little gathering of people who met in an upper room over a grocery store; and I remembered how that little church grew and struggled. I called to mind the difficulties under which it labored, how through a decade and a half, it could scarcely be said to stand on its feet; in fact, I really think we are "creeping" yet; still, although, during the first fifteen years we struggled along, I am happy to say that, during the last five years, under one of the best of leaders, we have been brought by our Master into green pastures; and, by contrast, we are in luxury where before we were in want. And, sir, as I have thought of our experiences, my mind went back to that little band which, over two hundred and fifty years ago,—I believe in 1608,—started out from that little English village of Scrooby and went up to the historic town of Leyden, and, not finding that large liberty of conscience which they sought, decided that they would come over to these New England shores; here they found what they desired; at least, if they did not find that complete freedom to the extent that they wished, we have found it to-day, and richly enjoyed the same. And I call to mind how that little band separated in Massachusetts, and sent down here into the State of Connecticut those little colonies such as Stratford and Milford and Guilford; and I remembered, as I read over their history, how that band here fought and contended with the Indians; suffered internal strife, in the same way the little Olivet Church has done, having dissensions, to the extent of sending off a feeble branch to found another church; though in our case the dissentors had a little more independence of character; (the portion that withdrew, instead of founding a similar church, were so independent that they founded a Methodist Church;) and, as I contrasted these two churches I said to myself, certainly, if out of so small a beginning, if out of so weak a church in numbers and influence, our mother church became so powerful, and has sent forth into this world heroic characters that are to-day building up both character for themselves and for the community; if this mother church of ours has become such a power in the world, and accomplished so much good, sir, your grandchild, weak as she is to-day, has a future before her, and we propose to fight along this line, and we propose to build up in that community where your grandchild exists, a God fearing and a God loving community. And, sir, when the roll shall be called two hundred and fifty years hence, I have no doubt that Olivet Church will be considered a worthy ancestor, as the blessed mother-church is to-day, and we perhaps may share in the celebration which shall be as blessed a re-union as this is to-day.

Mr. Ives. We have a baby, too, a few years old. We have reached the end of the list of the children, and now we are to hear from the baby. While this sword has been held over all the other speakers, I am delighted to say now to the baby, that she shall have full sway, and talk just as long as she wishes.

Response from the West End Church, Bridgeport.

Deacon J. W. Northrop.

I remember that one of the previous speakers prayed that God would have mercy upon the listeners.

In the name of the youngest grandchild, in the name of the West End Congregational Church of Bridgeport, I present to our dear venerable grandmother most hearty and affectionate greeting. We are the infant of the family, and we look for that special, loving attention, that always clusters about the baby. I have said we are the infant; for while our dear grandmother closes the wonderful cycle of two and a half centuries, we have fulfilled but two and a half years. And though an infant of so short a life, still it is no puny weakling, but a healthy, strapping, lusty child, fast striving toward maturity. The West End Congregational Church was recognized by a Council convened February 15, 1887. I have the honor to be one of the twenty-one original members of the church. Since that time we have added to our number sixty-three, and have lost six, having now a membership of seventy-eight, so that during the two and a half years we have quadrupled our numbers. If we continue to grow at this rate, for the two hundred and fifty years of our grandmother's life, we shall have a membership of—Well, I will not attempt to tell you how many. I began to figure it, and reached a million before I was fairly started, and I saw there was no use in figuring any farther, for what could we do with more than a million members? When we get up to a million there will be a little great-granddaughter born to our beloved grandmother; perhaps it will be a twin! But while we cannot truthfully say we expect to grow at this rate, we do look forward to a large increase in the future, for we are located at the West End; and the long headed, wise fellows say that from the very nature of things, the City of Bridgeport is bound to expand at the West End. And while a great many of those long headed fellows are real estate agents, they are not all real estate agents, so we put our confidence in what they say. The original enterprise from which the church sprang was a little Sunday-School mission work started by some good people in an unoccupied store. From the store we soon grew into a cottage where our fifty or sixty scholars were scattered through five rooms. Pupils sat on the stairs, others dangled their legs from the sink-board. From the cottage we grew into our present chapel-home with which our good mother, the First Church of Bridgeport so charitably clothed us. You must know that strapping infants are forever outgrowing their clothes. Last year's dresses won't button this year; the arms stick far out through the sleeves; the skirts cause us to smile at their shortness That is the trouble with this child, we can't keep inside of our clothes. Twice we have outgrown our garments, and now, the third time, we are in a ridiculous plight, pulling in our arms and drawing up our feet and afraid to take a long breath for fear of ripping a seam or bursting off a button! But we are not an indifferent youngster who had no regard for the fitness of things, and we propose to do something about it, and we propose to do a great deal about it. One feeble-kneed brother advocated ripping out the hems and patching down the old garments and trying to make them do. I am putting it very mildly when I say that that young man was simply *squelched*. No, my good friends, we have got to have another brand new set of clothes; and our hearts are already rejoicing in anticipation. We do not propose to cultivate our clothes at the expense of our souls and minds or even of our pockets, but we do realize the relative importance of pretty good clothes, at any rate, you feel tolerably comfortable inside of them. We have all taken measures in this direction, and, as everybody knows, taking measures is the first thing to do when you are to have a new set of clothes.

I have seen this Sunday-School work grow in numbers from twenty-five to two hundred, and now in truth we are in need of more commodious quarters in order to successfully carry on our work; but we trust that, before a very long time, we shall be in possession of a church building of ample size and accommodations to meet the needs of our enlarged work. God has indeed blessed us in the past. He has blessed us with this worthy grandmother, whose true piety and faith have without doubt had a benign influence over us. He has blessed us with a wise, affectionate mother, whose loving care has been around about us in the past, and who still cherishes us in a very tender place in her heart. Better than all, He has blessed us with His own divine presence. We have felt the influence, the joy of His overshadowing love, the power and grace of His good Spirit in our midst. And now, in closing, we pray that the God, who planted and has sustained throughout these centuries this dear grandmother church, will evermore bestow upon her His richest gifts; that throughout the coming generations she may continue a bright and shining light shedding abroad a clear radiance over the paths of multitudes of men; a fountain of the water of life from whence shall flow forth the streams that carry peace and joy and salvation to the hearts of the people.

MR. IVES. Let us close our services this afternoon by singing the 1141st Hymn. I desire to give two notices before singing the hymn. In the first place, of the relics which are upon exhibition in the lecture room at the rear of this house. The room will be open at the close of this service. The ladies have made ample provisions for a supper for all who can remain and be with us in the evening or for those who would take supper before returning to their homes. The supper will be served in the hall where the dinner was served, and the train is in no haste. You will be welcome at any time after half-past five. After singing, Mr. Davenport will pronounce the benediction, whom we are very glad to have with us to-day.

Hymn 1141. "Jesus shall reign where'er the sun."

BENEDICTION.

REV. J. G. DAVENPORT.

AND now may the blessing that maketh rich and addeth no sorrow, the blessing of God the Father, the Son, and the Holy Ghost, be upon us and upon all his Israel forevermore. Amen.

Congregational Church, Stratford, Conn.
Built in 1784 — removed and new Church built in 1859.

EVENING SERVICE.

Mr. Ives. Rev. Mr. Pardee, Rector of the Episcopal Church of this place, will now read the Scriptures.

Mr. Pardee. I will read the 55th Chapter of the Book of the Prophet Isaiah.

Mr. Ives. We will be led in prayer by my father, who preached in the building which preceded this one fifty-three years ago, and I have been happy to have him preach for me three times since I have been the pastor of this church.

PRAYER,

Rev. Alfred E. Ives, of Castine, Maine.

O Lord our God, we bow and worship before Thy face. We call upon our souls and all within us to praise and bless Thy holy name. Thou art faithful as the great mountains, that cannot be removed but endure forever. We rejoice in the manifestations of that faithfulness, in Thy dealings with Thy people here. We bless Thy name for this day, for this commemoration, that there is so much to commemorate, so much to recount with thankfulness and with joy. We praise and bless Thy holy name that in Thy providence and by Thy good spirit in years and generations gone the foundations of many generations here were laid in faith, in humble prayer. We rejoice that Thy watchfulness has been over this vine of Thy planting, that Thou hast caused it to bud and bring forth fruit so abundantly, extending its boughs to the sea and its branches to the river, that it has been like a bough, even a fruitful bough by a wall, whose branches ran over the wall. We rejoice that there have gone forth from this church other churches of Our Lord Jesus Christ, standing firm in the truth and love of God, blessed richly in the grace of God with enlargement and upbuilding and strength. We thank Thee for all Thou has done for this mother church and for those that have gone forth from her. We rejoice in Thy goodness and mercy to them, these churches of Jesus Christ, so much in them that manifest the faithfulness and love and power and grace of God. The Lord in His favor grant that, as in generations past, so in time to come, and more abundantly, the riches and grace of God may come to His people here, upon this church of God, upon all its membership, and upon all who are so closely related to it by that intimacy with it in the past. We pray that more and more Thou wilt work for Zion, that it may be every where made manifest that those who name the name of God are indeed a peculiar people, zealous of good works, the Lord Jesus dwelling with them in their hearts and in their habitations. We pray, Our Father, that in coming years there may still be enlargement from these churches, and that all these churches around about us and far away over this wide land may bear the name of Christ, and the riches of His grace be manifest in their enlargement. We thank Thee for all Thou has done for our land, and pray that more and more Thou wilt work until this land and all the lands shall be filled with the fullness and the grace of God. We commend Zion and her interests to Thee. Still thou dost work in the midst of the golden candlesticks. Still dost Thou carry the stars in Thy right hand, and with confidence we may commend our interests to Thee, and pray for Thy great name's sake Thou wilt work good unto them. Bless us in the remaining services of this evening, that they may be profitable to us and enjoyable to us and prove to Thy honor and glory, through Jesus Christ, our Redeemer. Amen.

Mr. Ives. It may perhaps be a relief to some if I give notice that the train for New Haven leaves at 9.21, and the train for Bridgeport at 9.26. We shall probably be through these exercises in abundant season for either of these trains, but if the services should be prolonged I will give notice, so that any who desire to take these trains may be amply notified.

Mr. Ives. I am very happy to announce an address from Dr. Hall, a former pastor of this church.

ADDRESS.

Rev. William K. Hall, D.D.

Mr. Moderator, Fathers and Brethren: I deem it a great privilege to be present with you to-day, and participate in this joyous festival, on this high day in the history of this ancient church. Though my pastorate was not a long one, it was sufficiently long for me to become thoroughly identified with the interests of this church, and to become intimately acquainted with many of you in your homes. It does not require a long time for a pastor to know his people by their firesides, to find his affections twining about many a home, forming the tenderest attachments with many hearts. Returning to-day after the lapse of eighteen years, a flood of memories has been sweeping through my mind, as I have met one and another and grasped the hand of those to whom I was so closely drawn years ago. I have been dwelling very much in the past.

But this is not the place or the hour for the utterance of thoughts which are for the most part of a private nature.

Our ears have become familiar with "Centennial" and "Bi-centennial," and no longer do we deserve the sneer that we have often heard from the other side of the sea, that we have no history, no monumental stones, that our life was young and callow. We are passing beyond that condition. We have been rapidly pushing on into events that have so crowded and crowned these years as to have made them some of the most important and conspicuous years, as far as the great interests of humanity are concerned, in all the world's history. I suppose that we may be apt to err in magnifying the relative value of the years immediately behind us as compared with the earlier centuries; and yet I think that, after the soberest reflection, one would conclude that the two hundred and fifty years, which span the life of this church, cannot be much surpassed in importance and conspicuousness, as regards the great vital interests of humanity, by any of the years or centuries that may yet come before the curtain drops and the great drama of history is closed. Already we are talking about the celebration of the Four Hundredth Anniversary of the discovery of America; but during the first hundred years and more of this period there was a comparative barrenness respecting any great important events that have a far outreaching influence upon the highest welfare of humanity. It is not until that period when the Pilgrims landed on the shores of Plymouth, one of the great epochs of history, and when the colonists laid these foundations of church and State along the shores of Connecticut, that we begin to strike the history that seems to be mighty in its every event, reaching far out down to the present and far on into the future. And so, when we review the history of this ancient church, looking backward two hundred and fifty years; when we come to you, dear brethren, as you stop in this grand, lordly march through the centuries halting for a little while to look back over the way by which you have come, we can feel with you that the fathers began their work at a period in the history of this world which in all probability will not be surpassed in all the years and centuries that are before us, for the gravity of the nature of the events in which they were the actors, and for the profound significance of the issues proceeding from them. It is a fact of great suggestive value, as it seems to me, that while we are celebrating our centennials and bi-centennials of civil government and civil institutions, there are simultaneously these church centennials. While we lift up our thanks to God for the government under which we have reached such great prosperity; for the civil and religious freedom that is our glorious inheritance from the fathers, we do not fail to come and bow lovingly and reverently at these holy shrines, at these church altars our fathers reared. We do not fail, I say: aye, we must do it if we are true to history. There is thus brought prominently before our minds the significant fact that coeval with the foundation of civil government were the foundations of these churches of Christ. This is a fact brought with great power by these commemorative celebrations upon the minds of the youth of this generation, even as it comes with great and refreshing power upon the minds of those in middle life and those who are passing away. And we are reminded by it that the source of this national prosperity, the primal cause of this blessedness that is ours under these civil institutions, must ever be inseparably linked with the House of God.

My friends, the question perhaps may come to some practical mind, of what utility are such church anniversaries as this which we are enjoying to-day? Of what value can they be to us or to our children? Is it not merely a passing sentiment, pleasing, it may be, for the hour, but leaving no abiding product of good behind it? Homer tells us that Diomede did not see the gods until Pallas Athene swept the mist from before his eyes. It is by the power of reminiscences such as these we have had to-day, that the mists are blown away from before our eyes. We look back along the path of this church history and see the consecrations to God, the fidelities to his service and the hallowed and hallowing genius and the profound religious spirit of the men who wrought for us in the years gone by. It is only by the power of just such memories as these revived to-day that we properly estimate the worth of those who laid the foundations of the goodly structure into which we have entered, and which has been and is our pride and our joy. Of what value to us? Value in the inspiration and impulse we receive for the re-consecrating of ourselves to a like service, of the quickening of our own faith in God, and in the building up in ourselves of a like moral strength, and a like righteous character. There was once a time when the Moabite soldiers prevented a burial, and they hastily cast the body into the sepulchre of Elisha; and the sacred writer tells us that when the body touched the old bones of Elisha it revived and stood upon its feet. It is by the touch that we have had to-day of this revered past of this history of God's Providence in this church, of that grace He gave to the fathers, that we ourselves are revived and anointed anew for the work that God has for us to do.

I have noted in the addresses that have been made to-day

that very little has been said of the talents, of the learning, of the great abilities of those who occupied in the earlier years the pulpit of this and of other churches that have sprung from it. Among them were great preachers, men of much learning, men foremost in intellectual strength and attainment of the time, but these points have not been emphasized to-day. Prominent in your thoughts and in the thoughts of those who have spoken to us, has been the spirit that possessed them, the faith that animated them, the consecration to God and His service that characterized their lives. There is helpfulness in this fact for us. For we, by the power of these memories thus revived, are greatly aided to see, that effective work for God, the fulfilling of our mission in the world, after all depend upon a right heart, upon a true spirit, upon consecration to God and His service. As we look back over the history of this church we are impressed with what numberless sacrifices and numberless fidelities must have marked those who have been prominent through all the years from the beginning of this church life. There is something rather wonderful, and yet very intelligible, Mr. Moderator, in this fact of a continued spiritual life, a fidelity of godliness for two hundred and fifty years. Whence came it? How has it been sustaind? Two hundred and fifty years of unbroken, continuous, indestructible holy life, a life of faith in Christ, a life of love for him, a life of fidelity to the Cross of Jesus! How shall we explain it except by the indwelling Spirit of God in human hearts, the Divine Spirit, touching this human life and that human life, lighting a flame here on this heart and there on that heart, and the flame ever burning brightly, the life once given continually sustained, through all these years. This truth was forced afresh upon my mind this morning, as obedient to the promptings of my heart, I visited yonder burying-ground and stood before the monument of one whom I had laid there to rest. I stood and pondered, and remembered, and prayed. I have but to mention the name of Deacon D. P. Judson, for all of you who were his contemporaries at once know that I speak the name of one who, if we could have looked into his heart, would, next to the name of wife and children, have written the name of this church of Christ. I remember him as one who was of unspeakable comfort and strength to me in the days of my pastorate of this church. I remember him as one who bore on his heart of hearts every interest of this church, and whose unselfish devotion to its welfare was recognized by all. I make this reference merely for the sake of an illustration. That that one life was but one of many with which this church through all the years has been blessed. Each generation in turn has had many who, in steadfast faith, with believing prayer and unwearied labor have ministered at this altar. Here we have the explanation of the fact of this unbroken church life for two hundred and fifty years in this community. It has been and is the "Church of the living God." Brethren there are great souls behind us.

We, of to-day, who have entered into the privileges and blessings they have bequeathed to us; we who have the enjoyment of the successes and victories they have gained for us, have not begun to measure their heroism of thought, of feeling and of action; their numberless sacrifices; their numberless fidelities. If we are to be worthy of them we must gird the loins of our mind and be sober and earnest, and faithful to the end.

Not only has this continuity of church life in its inner spirit and power been strongly impressed upon me to-day. There is another; and it is that of the presentation of the faith once delivered to the saints,—loyalty to the standards of truth and to the forms and ordinances of the gospel. I would not have any of you infer that I believe that our fathers of two hundred and fifty years ago did the thinking for us of to-day. I would not have you suppose that I am so bigoted as to feel that we can make no improvement in the terminology of our religious creed. I would not have you for a moment think that I am so wedded to uninspired words, to mere forms and statements of truth that men have made, as to think that the expressions and utterances of one Christian age are sufficient for all time. But we may count as certainties to-day many things which our fathers would have regarded as wild dreams, while we may have wider and broader vistas of truth than they had. While the streams of truth have been growing wider and wider, and our bark may have been driven into broader and deeper harbors of knowledge, yet, still, let us remember to cultivate the spirit of reverence for the past, for only as we have reverence for the past can we have any hope for the future. While we have reverence for the past, let us be deeply humble as to what we ourselves have gained or may gain. Let us remember that though the paths we are treading may lead us into broader fields and open out into wider and more attractive vistas, that these paths are those the fathers marked out for us. We did not mark them out for ourselves. So, with profound gratitude for their work along all the lines of religious and theological life, of social life, of intellectual life, let us, in our rejoicings to-day, congratulate ourselves that such a noble lineage is ours. Let our congratulations be in a spirit that I can no better express to you than in the simple words of the familiar heart-touching hymn, "More love, O Christ, to Thee, more love to Thee." Let us lift up on high, as ours, the motto of the early Redemptionist Fathers, "All for Thee, dear Christ, All for Thee." And may the blessing of the God of the fathers, that rested upon the fathers, rest upon their children to the remotest generations.

We shall now have the pleasure of listening to a former pastor of this church, Rev. Mr. Fitch.

DENOMINATIONAL ESPRIT DE CORPS.

Rev. Frank S. Fitch.

Why is Protestant Christendom divided into so many sects? The Church of Rome answers confidently because of the great apostacy from the true church. Human reason was enthroned in the place of the authority of the apostles and their successors, and disintegration is the natural and necessary result. Behold the evils of dissent, say the State or established churches such as the Church of England.

A partial explanation is found in the fact that there were

various degrees of reformation in different localities. The movement throughout Western Europe was a general one, but modified in some degree at each separate center. All could agree that salvation is by faith and not by works, and that the Scriptures themselves and not the Pope or the church are the court of final decision, but the accepted doctrine of the right of final interpretation of God's word opened the way for differences of opinion in reference to the true significance of the Lord's Supper, the mode of baptism, the relation of church to state and the seat of ecclesiastical authority, and hence we find ourselves in this year of our Lord, 1883, strangely divided.

It is not hard to account for these existing differences. We know why they have been and are; our chief interest is in their future mutations. Is denominational spirit diminishing? Are the fences between the different estates of our Protestant churches being lowered from time to time, with a speedy prospect of final removal, as popular speech in our union conventions so often and confidently asserts? The ease and willingness with which pastors change from the care of churches of one polity to those of another, and the individual members find a new Christian fellowship, according to considerations of personal convenience or business and social interests would seem to answer—Yes.

There is, confessedly, a good deal of politeness. Our religious assemblies welcome fraternal delegates with great cordiality and abundant applause when they assure us that the points of agreement between our different denominations are many and important while our differences are few and nearly obsolete. Sermons whose substance is an attack upon the rival across the way are far less common or welcome than fifty years ago. The greater intelligence, wider observation and more kindly spirit of both our clergy and laity is noticeable; yet we must not forget that there are always counter currents. The Gulf Stream may flow continuously in one direction, but there is no massing of waters on the coasts of Britain or lack in the Gulf of Mexico. From one point of observation it may seem that denominational spirit moves only in warm currents with summer and harvest in its train, while from another the chill of party spirit and the shock of unholy competition first arrest attention. These icebergs from a clime where our Lord's kingdom has not been established float far into the blessed region of home and foreign missionary activity and sink many a gospel ship and drown many a brave and self-sacrificing servant of the Master.

Denominational schools and colleges are multiplying on every hand. Each considerable branch of the Protestant church has its educational, church erection, home and foreign missionary societies, and now great book concerns are providing Sunday-School papers, lesson leaves, weekly religious papers, monthly and quartely magazines.

Even the great national societies, whose accomplished work is second to none other in our century, in which the churches of our order have had such honorable place, the American Board, the American Home Missionary Society, the American Missionary Association, are now, in fact, denominational societies. Whose fault is it—ours? No! We desired coöperation, worked for coöperation, have given money, men and churches in our effort to secure coöperation. Our sincerity cannot be questioned. Is this a record of partial failure? No! but an honorable and permanent testimony. If we bear henceforth a denominational name, work by denominational methods, and have need of cultivating more denominational spirit, it is because our younger brothers and children have set up housekeeping for themselves and left us alone with our inheritance of national societies and colleges to maintain as best we may. Many of us do not regard the denominational life of Protestant Christendom, as now manifested, as the ideal or ultimate form of the visible church of Christ. It is too narrow and exact in doctrinal statement and too confident in ecclesiastical polity. Each branch is positive as to its own teachings and method. It seems to rest all, in true Protestant fashion, on the Scriptures; but Independents, Presbyterians, Methodists and Episcopalians cannot all and at the same time be *absolutely* apostolical and scriptural. Yet they seem to think so. They say so. I cannot believe that the unhealthful and unchristian spirit manifested but too often in the past in our home missionary work is necessary or needs any increase. Such are some of the evils of denominationalism, yet great as they are and much to be deplored, they are less than those of enforced conformity as our fathers knew and deplored them in England. They are incident to times of experiment and transition, and are already attracting attention. The long-talked-of and not much practiced comity between denominations in home missionary work, is beginning to be employed, not very generally, nor with remarkable enthusiasm, yet like Civil Service Reform and other things too good for half sanctified society, it is being demanded by the best thought and piety of the time, and the people will not rest until the work of Christ is done in his spirit and by methods which need no apology.

The rapid enlargement of our cities in the older States, the new empires opening for conquest and development in the New West and Southwest, and the open doors of the whole heathen world, invite men and societies to a nobler work than serving disaffected minorities or building churches for uneasy individuals who have pet theories which they wish to test chiefly by means of the *toil* and *gifts* of *others*.

What is the duty of Congregationalists at this time? Are we to yield the field forever, as our fathers did in hundreds of instances in the Empire State in times past, to our more confident and less scrupulous rivals through fear of showing a sectarian spirit; or are we to enter the lists of the denominational race for supremacy in this country and become the most boastful and saucy of the whole ignoble company?

I do not see any need of doing either. A healthful and honorable competition is better than an unchecked and irresponsible monopoly, whether we are engaged in carrying breadstuffs from Minneapolis to Liverpool, or transporting citizens from Connecticut to the New Jerusalem. There are now no "licensed carriers." The route which is shortest, cheapest, makes the best time and delivers its merchandise in the best condition will be the "poeple's line." The highest practical utility is the test. The great public is an interested and intelligent observer in this time of construction and competition. Should we have more denominational spirit? Can we hope to compete with rival and parallel trunk lines as a great continental agency? We say confidently, yes. Our line is the most direct, and least expensive, our machinery strong and simple, our stock has never been watered—try us. The creed maker is abroad. For some time he has been without occupation. In common with manufacturer, projector of railroads and merchant marine, he has been under a cloud. There has been no demand for his wares nor reverence for his person. So long as the fundamentals of church and state were questioned, and the very foundations of existing institutions were trembling, the defender of the faith like the resident of regions frequented by earthquakes has been content to dwell in a one-story house with very broad base, with a half preference to live wholly out of doors. He could not be threatened or cajoled into an admission that he believed anything in particular or had great attachment for the possessions of his fathers. But now how different. The maker of creeds in common with many others is thoroughly convalescent. His discouragement has vanished. His occupation, in his own judgment at least, is no mean one, and he is making active preparation for spring trade. From basement to loft all the wares of the port are being brought forth, remnants, unsaleable fabrics, dust-covered and faded patterns with here and there a novelty, are spread before the thronging crowd of purchasers with all the eagerness of an Israelite tradesman. All the creeds from the so-called Apostles' down to that of the National Council's Committee of Twenty-five are on exhibition. It is not strange that such a fascinating occupation as creed-making should have an early revival. It is just as delightful to make ecclesiastical raiment for the use of others as to provide gowns for the queen of fashion. Now I am not ambitious to make a creed out of new cloth, but as suggestions are invited I wish somewhere between the Apostles' Creed and to-morrow's to insert this single phrase—"I believe in the local church."

I *believe* in the *local church*. I believe that it has a Scriptural basis; although I do not insist that other ecclesiastical systems have not. For one, I am willing to admit that I do not find any one of the great branches of the Church catholic, Congregational, Presbyterian, Methodist Episcopal, Protestant Episcopal, Greek, or Roman Catholic, fully equipped in doctrine, discipline, and activities in its exact present form in the New Testament. All doubtless have their proof-texts, and with greater or less admixture of human opinion and error have developed their systems from the germs contained in Revelation. All I claim is that we rest our theory of the local church as complete in itself on what is written. To the law and the testimony is our friendly challenge. I regard our theory of the local church, as seen in our Congregational sisterhood, as a valuable working hypothesis. I am confident that the more severely accurate exegesis of the future, and the careful comparative study of the relative excellence of the many outward expressions of Christianity in church life to which, whether they consent or not, all systems are being subjected, will require of us as few changes as of any other, and we have no such superstitious reverence for the mere words or methods of the Fathers, Reformer or Separatist, Puritan or Pilgrim, as to be unwilling to make any modifications, which may be proven to be required by God's word. I believe that our churches are true churches of our Lord Jesus Christ. We have tried, whether with entire fidelity or not, we may not judge, to reproduce the New Testament churches. I believe in our local self-governed churches because of their quickening influence in secular life.

They have cultivated no monastic spirit nor sought escape from the burden of affairs.

They have been in spirit and in fact in the world but not of it.

Burke, in the House of Commons, says Dr. Dexter, once remarked: "Their way (*i. e.*, the Colonists') of professing religion accounts for their fierce love of liberty."

The town meeting and the local church have been the schools of an intelligent patriotism and a thoughtful piety. That each community, however small, must have the care of many of the great interests of men, in matters both temporal and spiritual, busying itself continually with facts, theories, hindrances and measures, is vital to the purity and permanence of our institutions.

These deliberations may be often unbusiness-like and petty in comparison with the legislation of parliaments and the findings of councils, but we must not forget that our growing numbers and widening domain increase the tension upon each individual community, and make new demands for personal intelligence and honor. These come from study, observation and responsibility. Mere assent and conformity never have nurtured men. Personal interest, personal care, personal honor, constant search for truth and unselfish loyalty to it when discovered must not pass away in the land of the Pilgrims.

I believe in the local church because of its adaptation to the work of the future. It is flexible, uses generals to meet particulars, willingly allows time, the remorseless pruner, to cut away much of last year's woody structure now that its fruit has been garnered, that it may be able to bring forth more abundantly. It remembers that only the new wood buds, blossoms, and bears fruit. The old may serve as supports, as anchorages to the past. The leaves, in closest contact with air and sunlight, most sensitive and eager, must eat, digest, assimilate, and even envelop the venerable part with one layer more to increase its bulk, its weight and its value. This new layer must be itself all the time the most thoroughly alive part of the tree, serving as pipes for the sap-currents, as levers to open the clinging bark, that a large life may be possible; and if now and then a portion be sloughed off it is no matter.

The youth of the future will not break with the Bible. Nothing has been found to take its place. They will not deny Christ. There is none other name whereby we must be saved. They will not cease to use the winnowed grain of other days, but they have no use nor taste for husks.

A revised edition of the English Bible, more Biblical statements of Christian dogma, more manuals of Christian songs, enlarged methods of Christian service, a better understanding among Christians as to practical philanthropy, more of comity between the Protestant denominations in home missionary work, a better temper and more intelligent attitude toward what is best in modern scientific thought, a revival of practical righteousness, a fine sense of personal honor in all the complex relations of modern life that shall compel the respect and secure the imitation of all beholders because the spirit of this world never has, never can counterfeit it, a consecration of the wealth and culture of these days of prosperity and peace which shall equal in measure and quality the sacrifices of the Fathers and make us able to catch the spirit as well as repeat the words of their prayers and confessions,—such are some of the demands made upon the church of Christ in our day, demands which I need not say in this presence are reasonable, earnest, imperative. We must meet them or the fire which will try every man's work will find nothing in the edifices built by this self-sufficient generation but wood, hay and stubble easily consumed and leaving as a residue only ashes.

Can the churches of our order do a part of this needed work for which the world waiteth? I believe that they can, that their history, their equipment is inferior to none; that they have the courage to fight again if needs be on historic fields, and the zeal to press eagerly into new regions.

Mr. Ives. We now have the pleasure of an address from Dr. Henry M. Booth. I do not know as his name appears upon our church roll, but his father was for many years a member of the church, and others of the family have been members here. We are glad to welcome him.

THE GERMINAL PRINCIPLES OF THE PILGRIMS.
Rev. Henry M. Booth, D.D.

There is but one reason why I should speak at this time, and that reason suggests an appropriate theme. From the first day until now, men of my name and blood have been members of the church of Stratford. In the year 1641, Mr.

Richard Boothe, an honored ancestor, was here, as an active participant in public affairs, and there is no reason to doubt that he was present, also, in 1639, when this organization was effected. My father, Mr. William A. Booth, and my uncle, Mr. Charles H. Booth, whose hoary heads are crowns of glory, as they are found among us still in the way of righteousness, were instrumental in the erection of the beautiful Sanctuary, which has opened its doors to receive this interesting celebration. The bright, summer days of my own childhood were familiar with the river and the brooks, the meadows and the forests, which seem to have been made, by our considerate Father in Heaven, for the especial happiness of an active boy.

I am here, therefore, in a representative attitude. The church of Stratford has a right to claim my presence; and I am honored by the courteous invitation, which has given me this opportunity of speech.

As descendants of the Pilgrims, we revere the intelligence, the virtue and the piety, which have made our life a possibility. Those principles were germinal. Other men labored, and we have entered into their labors. Ours is the harvest, while theirs was the seed-time. Degeneracy is not evident; but progress. The past is never honored by insisting upon the immorality and irreligion of the the present, the decline of integrity and the prevalence of vice. It is to the credit of the husbandman that his planting yields an hundredfold. The flinty seed is a prophecy, which the full corn in the ear must interpret. Until experience becomes a teacher, no one can imagine whereunto this strange thing will grow. "That which thou sowest, thou sowest not that body that shall be, but bare grain, it may chance of wheat, or of some other grain, but God giveth it a body, as it hath pleased him, and to every seed his own body." It is so with principles. Men discover them, and announce them. They drop into the soil of human nature, where they germinate. The future exhibits their quality in freedom, law, and godly living; and then turns back to crown the wise men, who aforetime went forth weeping, bearing precious seed.

This then is our conviction. The former days were not

better than these. We do not wish to exchange 1889, in any particular, for 1639. A decade of life now means more than a half century did then. We have a wider out-look, a more generous sympathy, a clearer intelligence, a stronger faith— and this is true, because the Pilgrims were the men of God's selection, who crossed the broad Atlantic with important germinal principles.

But what were these principles? We may name but two, although there were many others. Two, however, were especially prominent in the great and decisive struggle of Puritanism, which explains the migrations of the Pilgrims The divine authority of the Holy Bible, and the right of personal liberty in the sight of God were beliefs, which these heroic men held against arguments and threats and persecutions in the old world. To them the Holy Bible was the direct message of Almighty God. They accepted it without compromise. It was the one—and often the only—volume in their dwellings. They read it at the firesides, during the long, cold, desolate winters; and they talked about it to their children and neighbours until its historical facts and sublime doctrines had taken complete possession of their minds. "To its pages," says Mr. John Fiske in his recent valuable essay on the "Beginnings of New England," "they went for daily instruction and comfort, with its strange semitic names, they baptized their children, upon its precepts, too often misunderstood and misapplied, they sought to build up a rule of life that might raise them above the crude and unsatisfying world, into which they were born." We smile, as we read some of their interpretations. We wonder, as we find them trying to reproduce in New England the mistaken Judaism of the time of our Lord. But they were at work in a rich quarry. They were advancing along safe lines. Immortal principles, long buried out of sight, long neglected by a lazy and a despotic priesthood, were discovered, and, later generations, enlightened by the Holy Spirit, could be trusted to separate the gold from the quartz, and to survey and map out the newly discovered territory. Thus it came to pass that loyalty to the Holy Bible expressed itself, in 1636, by an appropriation of

£400, which the General Court of Massachusetts voted towards the establishment of a college at Newtown—"the first body in which the people by their representatives ever gave their own money to found a place of education"—and in 1639, in the Hartford Constitution, which "was the first written constitution known to history that created a government." Thus biblical truth secured an early prominence, in education and in politics, whose influence is still manifest, as, at this hour, great and distant territories are organizing to become States of the Republic.

But personal liberty was cherished by the Pilgrims with an intensity, which matched their reverence for the Holy Bible. They would call no man Lord. The heart-searching Judge of all the earth was recognized, as the only Lord of the conscience. They gave up home and friendships to be free. They were, it is true, not as tolerant as they might have been. Liberty was personal, rather than social. They had not learned to measure other men by the Golden Rule, as they expected themselves to be measured. Differences of opinion awakened bitter antagonisms. They could not agree with Quakers and Episcopalians; and they believed that they were discharging a duty, when they put an unsympathetic visitor into the streets. Roger Williams held views, which are now the views of most Christian patriots in our country; and so liberal a man, as Governor Winthrop, advised Williams that it would be safe for him to make his home among the Indians. No harsh judgment, however, need be passed upon this narrowness. Catholicity was a stranger to those times Indeed, we are just beginning to form an acquaintance with a genuine Catholicity. We do not burn and stone one another it is true, and yet our words are sometimes as hot as a flame, and as rough as brick-bats. We are still learning. Two hundred and fifty years have taught many lessons to an appreciative Christendom. Freedom of speech is the safety-valve, which has prevented frequent explosions. Gas is never very dangerous, if it is allowed to escape into the air. When it is confined, it threatens life and property. My claim to personal liberty covers your claim to the same inestimable privilege: and if I demand that you should respect my freedom of conviction, so long as I behave myself in a lawful and an orderly manner, you may make similar demands of me. Thus toleration may become social liberty in all parts of this broad land.

Holding firmly to these principals, our fathers, here in Stratford, associated themselves with the Hartford, or Connecticut Colony which was then more liberal in its attitude than the nearer Colony of New Haven, in which none but church members were allowed a participation in the privileges of citizenship. They were husbandmen, whose planting the generations have honored. The history of the church of Stratford is the abundant harvest, which we now contemplate with gratitude to God, and with admiration for his servants, our ancestors. But the end is not yet. Seed-time has not gone by forever. We, too, have duties, which are comparable to theirs. The principles which we have received, are capable of further development. The Holy Bible is not exhausted. John Robinson's memorable remark about its contents is still in order. Liberty has grander triumphs to record. We are in the line of a noble succession. Those who come after us, may rise up, and call us blessed. Let us thank God for the opportunity! Let us address ourselves to the rare and sacred privilege!

On the famous rock at Plymouth in the Commonwealth of Massachusetts, a splendid monument was recently dedicated with impressive ceremonies. More than two centuries and a half had passed since the Pilgrims left the Mayflower and landed upon those shores. To commemorate the principles of that distinguished ancestry, the Plymouth monument is to stand through the centuries. Upon a granite pedestal, a sculptured figure of Faith is raised. In her left hand, there is an open Bible, while with her right hand she points upward, to the divine source of all true inspiration. At her feet are statues of Education, Law, Morality, and Freedom—all reverently submissive to her firm, yet gentle authority. "Honored names are on the pedestal, and sculptured tablets represent the chief scenes of their career, the embarkation, the compact, the landing, and the first treaty with the Indians; but overshadowing all are the embodiments of those immutable principles, which lifted them above the level of their privations and disappointments, and enabled their heroic spirits to soar with serene and constant poise in the higher atmosphere of faith and hope."

The conception of the artist, so grandly expressed in granite language is an eloquent tribute to the Pilgrims and a suggestive lesson to their children. The faith, which studied the Holy Bible, and referred the interests of daily life to Him, who guides and judges righteously, delayed not to establish Education and Law, Morality and Freedom, in every new community, which found a home on the banks of broad rivers, or in fertile valleys, or even amidst the forest shades. Faith in God and in the Word of God secured these inestimable blessings, when as yet the struggle for existence was a desperate conflict. The seed was planted, and the promise of the harvest seemed far away. But faith looks into the future. The distant is real, and often visible to faith. The Pilgrims were living for those, who should come after them. They left the impress of a holy faith upon institutions, which are essential to a civilized life. Theirs was the grand initiative; ours is the wise development: later centuries will enjoy the complete fruition. Elementary work at the beginning; careful discipline in the process; a splendid order at the end.

Education: A simple school-house then, commanding universities now; a few books donated by Christian ministers then, the precious treasures of immense libraries in every considerable town now; a few studies then, divinity, medicine and law, the professions of learned men, a wealth of science and art and literature now, with men of learning in every important vocation; instruction by teachers and ministers of religion then; instruction now by the press in every use of the printed page. A marvellous advance! A progress almost incredible! Look, with the eyes of John Harvard, who in 1638 left his library and the half of his estate to the feeble college at Newtown; and then look with your own eyes at that college, now the University of Cambridge, with its corps of instructors, and its roll of students, and its magnificent history! What shall the future be? What is before education in the coming years? Who can predict? Certainly, there will be wisdom and safety in holding education in subordination to Faith, where it was placed by the Pilgrims in the early years. An education, which considers all knowledge, and then brings its treasures to a Faith, whose gaze is Godward, is the pledge of the finest product of civilization, the perfect man in the likeness of Jesus Christ. With you and with me, the active men of the present generation, rests a result, so desirable. Let us be faithful!

Law: Justice administered by council and governor then, by an alliance of church and State; justice, conserved to-day by the most august tribunal in the world—the Supreme Court of the United States—from whose decisions there is no appeal, and seldom a desire to appeal. What shall the future be? Shall the dignity of law be maintained and increased? Is it possible to make respect for law equal to standing armies and large companies of police? Can we hope that law, among a free people, will exercise so powerful an influence that offences will cease, and prisons will become useless? Surely, we shall be assisted in this desirable endeavor, if Faith has a recognized supremacy, in which the authority of the heart-searching God is impressed upon the citizen. Law may subdue the lawless, and record its triumphs in a virtuous social order, and then offer to Faith, whose gaze is Godward a happy people, whose God is the Lord. With you and with me, the active men of this generation, Law finds its dependence. Let us be faithful!

Morality: Stern, rigid, uncompromising then, more gentle, sympathetic, pervasive, yes, and Christ-like now. The gain is evident. The morality of to-day is not an easy expediency, which finds honesty the best policy and so is honest: but it is an integrity, a purity, a catholicity, a nobility, which has never been equalled since the Sermon on the Mount was preached. This we affirm in the face of a complaisant pessimism, which is fond of criticizing public men and public measures, while abundantly satisfied with personal merit and individual attainment. But criticism can never be judicious, if it finds honesty only by standing before a looking-glass, and iniquity always by going to the window to observe the crowded street. But while we thus speak, we are not content. Who can ever be content, if it is possible to be better than we are? Morality calls for self-denying effort. There is much to be done. Faith must rule. God must become the authority. The Decalogue is a Statute-Book of perpetual obligation. Happy will it be for us, if our morality shall be so intimately associated with Faith, whose gaze is Godward, that the pressure of a divine obligation shall be felt, and the hope of a divine approval shall become an inspiration. With you and with me, the active men of this generation, rests the morality of the coming years. Let us be faithful!

And *Freedom:* what shall we say of freedom? The Fathers believed in a freedom, which has written many a dark and distressing chapter of our nation's history. Our freedom is an advance upon theirs. We rebuke persecution: we call no man a slave: we frown upon bigotry: we welcome the oppressed. Yet freedom, in many quarters, is the synonym of license; and in many others, it is only a name, which covers cruel bigotry and wicked deeds. We have yet to present to the world a Freedom, which is the expression of Education, Law, and Morality; a Freedom, which utters its "Our Father" in daily prayer, and then considers "Our Brethren" in daily conduct; a Freedom, which looks up to Faith, whose gaze is Godward, and confesses that in the Holy Bible is to be found the liberty, wherewith Christ makes free. Thus the suggestion of the Fathers awaits its clear interpretation in the associated life of a great nation, whose strength and wealth are the evident dangers of an unexampled prosperity. To you and to me, the active men of this generation, God has committed this great trust. Let us be faithful, so that our fellow-men, in later years, may enjoy a Freedom, which will prove a perfect brotherhood.

Thus we stand at the close of the years, so memorable. Looking back, we salute the honored sires, whose names we reverence, and whose deeds we prize: looking about us, we exhort our fellow-men, whose toil we share and whose fellowship we now enjoy: looking onward, we hail the generations yet unborn with promise and with hope, pledging them the safe transmission of the fathers' principles, not as glittering gems, the same to-day as when first discovered, but as precious seed, planted and re-planted, and planted still again to support the life of man upon the earth and ever to yield a planting for those who will be here in other years.

The scene, brighter now than it was two hundred and fifty years ago, will be brighter two hundred and fifty years hence than it is to-day—and in this place, as elsewhere, the Lord of Life and Glory shall come, responsively to Faith, to pronounce his commendation upon Education, Law, Morality, and Freedom, as exhibited in the land to which the Pilgrims brought their germinal principles.

> "Down the dark future, thro' long generations,
> The echoing sounds grow fainter, and then cease,
> And like a bell, with solemn, sweet vibrations,
> I hear, once more, the voice of Christ say, ' Peace.'
>
> ' Peace,' and no longer from its brazen portals
> The blast of war's rude organ shakes the skies,
> But beautiful as songs of the immortals
> The holy melodies of love arise."

Mr. Ives. Even the brightest day draws to its close; and so these most delightful exercises must be concluded. Let us join in singing the 155th hymn, after which the benediction will be pronounced by Mr. Holden, of the Olivet Church, Bridgeport.

BENEDICTION.

Rev. E. K. Holden.

And now may the Lord bless you and keep you. The Lord make His face shine upon you and be gracious unto you. The Lord lift upon you the light of His countenance and give you peace. Amen.

ILLUSTRATIONS.

Congregational Church, Stratford,	Frontispiece.
Church Decorations, Looking West,	9
Interior of Old Church,	38
Collation Tables at Town Hall,	45
Church Decorations, Looking East,	76
Old Congregational Church,	92
Collection of Relics in Lecture Room,	82

NOTE.—The Committee on Publication are indebted to F. C. Leach, Esq., for photographs, and to Deacon R. B. Lacey for electrotype used in illustrating this book.

CONTENTS.

	PAGE.
Address, Historical, Rev. J. S. Ives,	16
Of Welcome, Rev. J. S. Ives,	47
Rev. William K. Hall, D.D.,	95
Rev. Frank S. Fitch,	100
Rev. Henry M. Booth, D.D.,	107
Anniversary Hymn, Rev. J. S. Ives,	11
Benediction, Rev. J. S. Ives,	44
Rev. John G. Davenport,	90
Rev. E. K. Holden,	115
Committees, List of,	5
Communion,	42
Greeting to the Children, etc., Rev. William K. Hall, D.D.,	48
Rev. Frank S. Fitch,	52
Prayer, Rev. G. F. Prentiss,	12
Rev. C. R. Palmer, D.D.,	13
Rev. William K. Hall, D.D., (Communion),	42
Rev. Frank S. Fitch, (Communion),	43
Rev. H. A. Davenport, (Blessing, Collation),	45
Rev. G. W. Judson,	46
Rev. Alfred E. Ives,	93
Programme,	7
Reading of Scriptures, Rev. J. A. Freeman,	13
Rev. Charles L. Pardee,	93
Response, Woodbury South, Rev. J. A. Freeman,	50
First Church Bridgeport, Rev. C. R. Palmer, D.D.,	55
Newtown, Rev. J. P. Hoyt,	57
Huntington, Rev. A. J. Park,	61
Trumbull, H. L. Fairchild, Esq.,	62
Monroe, Dea. W. Wells Lewis,	65
Southbury, Rev. David C. Pierce,	67
Bethlehem, Rev. J. P. Trowbridge,	69
Washington, Dea. E. W. Woodruff,	71
South Britain, Mr. John Pierce,	74
Woodbury North, Rev. J. L. R. Wyckoff,	76
South Church, Bridgeport, Rev. R. G. S. McNeille,	79
Park Street, Bridgeport, Rev. H. C. Hovey, D.D.,	82
Olivet, Bridgeport, J. J. Rose, Esq.,	85
West End, Bridgeport, Dea. J. W. Northrop,	87

www.ingramcontent.com/pod-product-compliance
Lightning Source LLC
Chambersburg PA
CBHW030404170426
43202CB00010B/1477